UPPARK
AND ITS PEOPLE

MARGARET MEADE-FETHERSTONHAUGH

AND

OLIVER WARNER

INTRODUCTION BY MARTIN DRURY

THE NATIONAL TRUST

First published in 1964 by George Allen & Unwin
© John Meade 1964
© Introduction The National Trust 1995

New edition published 1995
by National Trust Enterprises Ltd
36 Queen Anne's Gate, London SW1H 9AS

Printed in Great Britain by Clays Ltd, Bungay, Suffolk

A CIP catalogue record for this book is available from the British Library.

ISBN 0-7078-0194-x

CONTENTS

INTRODUCTION

This little book first appeared more than thirty years ago. Written by a distinguished naval historian, it concludes with an epilogue by Margaret Meade-Fetherstonhaugh, the last chatelaine of Uppark, who many years before had come upon the papers on which the book draws, damp and decayed, in a chest in the long-disused estate office, The first edition was privately printed and dedicated to her husband, Admiral Sir Herbert Meade-Fetherstonhaugh, who had inherited Uppark in 1931 under the terms of the will of a lady he had barely known and who had died when he was a boy.

There are few country houses in England that make such an appeal to the imagination as Uppark. Its situation, high and isolated on the crest of the South Downs, is as romantic and, for a seventeenth-century house, as unexpected as its story. Indeed, there is nothing about Uppark that is commonplace and little in its circumstances or its history that finds an echo in those of other country houses. Apparently remote from the business of the world, it is yet hardly an hour from London. Its tall south-facing windows command a panorama of tumbled downland stretching to the Solent and the distant Isle of Wight, and yet unseen below a ridge lies the city of Portsmouth. From outside Uppark has the simple charm and symmetry of a dolls' house, and yet the beauty of its interiors and the quality of the works of art they contain rival those in many more famous houses.

In nearly two hundred and fifty years Uppark has never been sold, and only twice has it passed between owners related to one another. Although it has stood in the wings of history, names familiar to every schoolchild have played brief parts in its serenely uneventful story. Long the home of an old landed family, it was the inspiration for a celebrated passage by H.G. Wells, extolling the role of the country house in the advance of human affairs. Until 1989 a benchmark of eighteenth-century taste, it was for a critical half-century the home of a dairymaid and her sister. When at last some of its precious contents had to be sold, they were lost at sea – as tradition has it, in the hold of the *Titanic*.

These are some of the threads that are woven into the story of *Uppark and its People*, but until the great fire of August 1989 the one on which visitors to Uppark most frequently remarked was the extraordinary completeness of its preservation. Sir Harry

Fetherstonhaugh died at a great age in 1846. In homage to his memory his widow, the dairymaid, and her sister made only superficial changes during their tenure which lasted until 1895. Much of the estate and some of the contents were sold during the life-tenancy of Colonel the Hon. Keith Turnour-Fetherston-haugh, but he and his wife, being already well into middle age when they succeeded, had no wish to make changes. The pro-ceeds of the sales had anyhow to be spent on repairing the roof rather than on modernising interiors. Thus it was that in 1931, when Sir Herbert and Lady Meade at last came into their inheri-tance, Uppark presented an extraordinary spectacle: a seven-teenth-century house whose eighteenth-century rooms had been preserved from modernisation by a combination of reverence, inertia, poverty and nearly a century of immunity from the reforming zeal of young wives. But, Uppark's luck held. Admiral Meade, who added the name of Fetherstonhaugh in 1932, was not a rich man; more significantly, his wife's imagination was immedi-ately caught by the beauty of the old house and by the poignancy of its condition. The epilogue which she appended to this book is testimony to a love affair with Uppark which began in 1931 and endured to the end of her life.

Lady Meade-Fetherstonhaugh, or Lady Fetherston, as she liked to be called, was a conservationist long before the word assumed the meaning it has today. Her instinctive response to Uppark was to hold it as she found it and to renew and replace only when conservation failed. To meet the need of the hour there came into her life Mrs Antrobus, the 'little old lady' referred to in this book. Mrs Antrobus was a herbalist who prescribed rinsing in an infu-sion of soap-wort as the means of rejuvenating the curtains and bed-hangings that were everywhere in listless shreds. This humble plant, which grows still at Uppark, acquired in Lady Meade's est-imation an almost mystical efficacy as curtain after curtain was rinsed, laid out on the lawn to dry and then carefully stitched on to a new backing by the little court of seamstresses she gathered around her. Guests, too, were enlisted in the great task and progress was recorded in her diary: 'October 25th 1934. Red letter day... washed the 1st saloon curtain & dried it in the Portico & then in the Stables as a gale was blowing. October 26th. Dried the white saloon curtain in the sun. It gleamed beautifully.'

Discoveries were made in attics and disused bedrooms: 'May 8th 1931. Went with Jim up into the Bedrooms above the Old

Kitchen & found in the Cook's bedroom the missing pair of white linen quilted bed curtains . . . . They were perfectly filthy & rain had poured in on them. A live bat was hanging in the folds of one . . . .'

Porcelain, silver, furniture, manuscripts, were joyfully discovered, dusted off, repaired and returned to use. The humblest object was hallowed by the accident of association with her beloved Uppark. In a drawer to this day are small pieces of card pierced by rusty pins and labelled in Lady Meade's firm hand: '18th-century pins. Do not throw away.'

In 1945, the war over and future uncertain, the Admiral and his son, Richard, approached the National Trust with the offer of Uppark and land to protect its setting as a gift to the nation. The Trust's files covering the next nine years are very fat, evidence of the determination of both parties to find a means of endowing the gift, and of the complexity of the resulting negotiations. But Uppark's guardian angel was still at his post. An endowment was put together comprising grants from the Pilgrim and Dulverton Trusts, the gift of some standing timber from the Admiral, and a large sum from an anonymous lady who had never seen the house, but whose generosity had been stimulated by a description given over the telephone by a member of the Trust's staff. And so, in 1954 Uppark passed to the National Trust.

The Admiral died in 1962. His widow remained at Uppark for a further six years before relinquishing the tenancy to her son's widow, Mrs Richard Meade-Fetherstonhaugh, and her young family. At her last home in the nearby village of Selborne, Lady Meade carried on her textile conservation, using the experience gained at Uppark for the benefit of historic textiles from other country houses. She died at Selborne in 1977.

Uppark is seven miles from the nearest fire station and for two hundred years depended for its water supply on the erratic performance of a ram which raised what it could from a pond at the foot of Harting Hill. The fear of fire was thus ever present and those who attended Lady Meade's Christmas parties for the children of Harting recall that, as she handed out presents from beneath the huge candle-lit tree set up each year in the hall, it was the Admiral's duty to stand by with a wet sponge on the end of a stick, ready to douse the candles when they burned low.

Twelve years after Lady Meade's death her apprehension proved well founded. On 30 August 1989 at about 3.30 in the afternoon visitors walking in the garden were horrified to see smoke billowing through the slates on the roof. Minutes before, a workman using a blowlamp to shape new lead flashings above the exterior cornice had just climbed down for his tea. The alarm sounded, the fire brigade arrived within fifteen minutes and, with the help of room stewards, members of the public, the Meade-Fetherstonhaugh family and an officer of the Grenadier Guards who chanced to be riding by on his horse, removed almost all the contents of the show rooms on the ground floor. But the flames burning inside the roof space were fanned by a strong wind from the south-west and the supply of water was hopelessly inadequate to control them. By midnight the upper two floors, the homes of two families, were destroyed and Sir Matthew Fetherstonhaugh's serenely beautiful sequence of eighteenth-century state rooms, criss-crossed with a cat's cradle of charred and fallen beams, stood a metre deep in a sodden black steaming porridge of ash and rubble.

In the days that followed there were those who urged the National Trust to raze what the fire had not consumed and return the site to nature. Others took the view that it should be consolidated as it was and reopened to the public as a roofless shell. Some, in deference to the shade of William Morris, pronounced that Uppark should be repaired in a contemporary idiom as a mark of confidence in our own times.

The Trust gave thought to all these options, but, devastating though the extent of the damage had been, it soon became apparent that much more survived than had at first been thought. The exterior walls of weathered pink brick were more or less unmarked. The floors and large expanses of wall in the principal rooms, with their fine plasterwork, carved woodwork and early nineteenth-century paint surfaces, survived. Careful sifting of the rubble produced fragments of rococo plasterwork from the fallen ceilings, the shattered remains of two cut-glass chandeliers, brass door furniture, two eighteenth-century lanterns, and much else that could be repaired or used as models for replacement. In addition, almost all the works of art, furniture, porcelain and many of the textiles from the state rooms had been salvaged intact. A photographic record of the interiors had been made some years previously, making accurate restoration possible. The house was, moreover, fully insured but for reinstatement only.

For these reasons the National Trust's decision was to treat Uppark as if it were a damaged work of art, to repair what could be repaired and to return it, inside and out, and as far as practicable, to its appearance before the fire.

The five-year campaign of repair that followed this decision is a story that cannot be told here. It drew on the skills and experience of many hundreds of people: architects, engineers, quantity surveyors, archaeologists, conservators, practitioners in many crafts, and all the building trades. It called for the revival of skills, such as free-hand modelling in lime-hair plaster, that had not been practised in England for more than a century. Above all, it demonstrated that in the age of technology the highest standards of craftsmanship in the working of natural materials can still be achieved.

Uppark is healed and stands once again alone on the Downs, smiling and confident, looking south to the sea. There are some hard edges, but time will soften them. And if in fifty years' time visitors still warm to the old house as they have for three hundred years, and if the fire appears to them as no more than one episode in its long history, the National Trust will have achieved its aim. It will have kept faith with the Admiral and his son, who gave the house to the nation, and with Lady Meade, who was for so long its devoted custodian.

Martin Drury
30 December 1994

I

The Fords and
the Building of Uppark

Uppark, a house set high on the South Downs above the Sussex village of South Harting, is a place very much on its own, not only by reason of its position, isolated, well chosen, yet not remote, but from its unusual history. A series of chances have ensured that this, one of the loveliest buildings of the late seventeenth century, has been cared for, and its furnishings preserved, in a way to which it would be hard to find a parallel.

In the course of over two centuries and a half, Uppark as it is visible today has had, in effect, only seven owners who have made it their principal home: Lord Grey of Werke, for whom it was built in the reign of William and Mary; the Georgian Sir Matthew Fetherstonhaugh, who bought it from Lord Grey's heirs, and who, with the help of his wife, re-modelled and decorated the interior; Sir Henry Fetherstonhaugh, who added a little to the fabric, on the suggestion of Humphry Repton, and much to the contents; his wife, once his dairymaid, who preserved it throughout much of the Victorian era, and her sister, to whom she left it; Colonel Keith Turnour Fetherstonhaugh, a life-tenant; and the present occupiers, who came into possession of the house in 1931 and who, nearly a quarter of a century later, handed over guardianship to the National Trust. Under Providence, Uppark can never now be spoilt, and what has been cherished for so long will continue in that state—the house not just preserved like a fly in amber, but lived in and enjoyed.

In the reign of Henry I the Lordship of the Manor of Harting was granted to the family of Hussey, who held lands in the neighbourhood for over five hundred years. They built Durford Abbey, which was given by the Crown to William Fitzwilliam at the time of the Dissolution of the Monasteries. Fitzwilliam alienated the lands to Henry Windsor, who in turn sold out to

Edmund Ford. The Fords, a prosperous family with extensive interests in the wool trade, came originally from Devonshire. Eight generations of descendants were to own the land on which Uppark is built, the proprietorship of Fords, Greys and Tanker-villes extending from 1546 to 1746—the last local interests of the Husseys being acquired in the reign of Elizabeth I.

During the stretch of time that Fords and Greys were in possession, one of their number, Edward Ford, descendant of the original purchaser, solved the problem of bringing an abundant supply of water from South Harting, which is itself 230 feet above sea level, to the site of the present house, which is 350 feet higher. His achievement enabled a mansion, with appropriate buildings, to be planned on a scale which would not have been practical if the occupants had had to depend on local dew-ponds and rain-water catchments. There had long been a dwelling at Uppark; masonry in the basement shows work which is at least as early as the sixteenth century. Edward Ford's ingenuity meant that far greater scope became possible, although there was no extensive building within his lifetime.

Edward Ford, son of William Ford, was born in 1605 and at the age of fifteen went to Trinity College, Oxford, as a Gentle-man Commoner. There he became a pupil of William Chilling-worth, a man only a little older than himself who was already making a name as a theologian of an anti-Puritanical cast. Ford's later career illustrates in a striking way how mistaken it is to conceive that any sharp line necessarily divided the fortunes of those who served the King's and the Parliamentary causes in what developed, during Edward Ford's middle life, into the English Civil War. He was a Royalist, on active service for Charles I from the opening moves of the war, but as events developed and the King was forced to abandon his attempt to win outright by force of arms, Ford was found useful by the other side. He survived the Commonwealth period, lived to be employed by Charles II after the Restoration, and left a name for technical ingenuity which gained him a place in the *Dictionary of National Biography*. Few contemporaries sur-mounted their troubles better, but that these were real and continued will be clear from a sketch of his life.

Soon after the outbreak of war, Edward was knighted by the King and appointed High Sheriff of Sussex. His father, Sir

William Ford, was alive, but it was plain to the Court that it was Edward who would be active for the royalist cause. Edward Ford was joined by Chillingworth, and they were both present at the taking of Chichester, in November 1642. A month later, at Haywards Heath, his men threw down their arms and made for home, and when the Parliamentarian General Waller later recaptured Chichester, Ford was among his prisoners. He was exchanged, possibly through the good offices of his wife, Sarah, who was the sister of Henry Ireton, one of the ablest Parliamentarians and himself to become Oliver Cromwell's son-in-law.

One of the feudal duties of the Lords of the Manor of Harting, laid down by a deed of the reign of Henry II, was to defend the castle of Arundel for the King in time of war. The provision had originally been drawn up more in anticipation of invasion than of Civil War, since Arundel was near the Channel coast, but Edward Ford was eager to fulfil his father's obligations in spite of earlier setbacks. The castle was in Parliament hands, but its garrison was weak, and the place was taken in December 1643 by Hopton and Ford without undue difficulty. Hopton then left Ford in charge, with men and provisions to withstand an attack. This soon came. In January 1644 Waller set to work in earnest and Ford was outmatched. The castle fell to Parliament once more and again Ford went as a prisoner to London. Chillingworth, who still accompanied him, did not long survive the reverse, while old Sir William Ford was seized at Uppark and marched off to London, presumably for complicity.

Although Sir William was soon exchanged, a Parliamentary Committee ordered Uppark woods to be cut down and sold, a bitter grief to the old man. 'Ye Petitioner humbly begs that Parliament wd not punish him for the Sonne's faults,' he wrote to the appropriate Commissioners, 'and is sorely aggrieved that . . . the Chichester Committee have caused many . . . Trees to be cut down close to his house which standeth upon a hill.'

Edward Ford had a longer spell as a prisoner after his Arundel failure than after Chichester, but when his exchange was at last arranged, he was still eager in the royal cause. In October 1645 he took part in the defence of Winchester Castle, but once again he was forced to surrender, and this time went to the Tower. Later he escaped abroad to join Queen Henrietta Maria in exile, where he was followed by his wife and daughter.

Edward had returned to England by 1647, when Charles was trying to negotiate terms with the Parliamentary army, for Clarendon, in his *History of the Rebellion*, mentions his efforts as a go-between in business with which Ireton had much to do. Clarendon remarks of Ford that he was 'a gentleman of good meaning, though not able to fathom the reserved and dark designs of his brother-in-law'.

Sarah Ford had meanwhile made use of her time by ensuring suitable matches for her daughter, Catherine. The girl married the Hon. Alexander Culpepper at the age of twelve, but the bridegroom died soon afterwards, and the widow was then united to Ralph Grey, son of the Speaker of the House of Lords in Charles's Parliament of 1643. Their eldest son, who was in time to become Lord Grey of Werke, was the builder of a new Uppark.

Edward Ford was employed by Oliver Cromwell in the improvement of the London water supply. Anthony à Wood, in his *Athenae Oxoniensis* says that he 'was a most ingenious mechanist, and being encouraged by Oliver and invited by the citizens of London in 1656, he raised the Thames water into all the highest streets of the city . . . to the wonder of all men, and the honour of the nation, with a rare engine of his own invention, done at his own charge and in one year's time'. The 'rare engine' included eight-inch pipes of Sussex iron.

Edward Ford's final 'ingenuity' was to plan a means of coining farthings distinguishable from one another, the idea being to avoid counterfeiting. He seems to have done the necessary work for his Patent in Ireland, though the idea came to nothing. He died, on September 3, 1670, his body being brought back to England and laid to rest in Harting church. He was commemorated by an arched tomb on the south side of the chancel.

Edward Ford's property devolved upon his daughter Catherine and upon her husband, who in 1674 succeeded to his father's barony of Grey of Werke. The northern estates included a Northumbrian castle at Chillingham, where the family spent much time. Ralph Grey enjoyed his title for one year only, and when he died he was succeeded by his son Ford. At that time Ford was twenty, and was a close friend of the Duke of Monmouth, Charles II's natural son by Lucy Walter. In the year of his succession he married Mary, fourth of the six daughters of

Lord Berkeley, not unaware that his bride had already found some favour with his friend, though the extent of their involvement is unknown. That their fondness for one another may have continued is suggested in a passage from a letter written on January 30, 1679, by the Dowager Countess of Sunderland.

'The Duke of Monmouth has so little employment in State Affairs that he has been at leisure to send two fine ladies out of town. My Lord Grey has carried his wife into Northumberland and my Lady Wentworth's ill eyes did find cause, as she thought, to carry her daughter into the country, in so much haste that it makes a great noise, and was done Sure in some great passion. My Lord Grey was long in believing the Duke of Monmouth an unfaithful friend to him. He gave her but one night's time to take leave, pack up and be gone.'

In default of a legitimate son to succeed Charles on the throne it was almost inevitable that the later years of his reign should be over-clouded with intrigues concerning the future. James, Duke of York, Charles's heir and brother, was a professed Catholic, and it was a view widely held in the country that a Catholic king was intolerable. Although Charles himself said of Monmouth, 'Much as I love him, I would rather see him hanged at Tyburn than I would confess him to be my heir', the young man had a deep seated ambition to become a Protestant king, and he made every use of his popularity, which was considerable, to further his own cause. He was often with Lord Grey at Harting, for he loved the chase, and he rode with the Charlton hounds, which were kennelled either at Uppark or nearby, showing himself more than once with Grey at Chichester and elsewhere on county Progresses.

Grey was concerned with every plot with which Monmouth's name was linked, but the escapade which first brought him notoriety had nothing to do with affairs of State. It concerned the seduction of his sister-in-law, Lady Henrietta Berkeley, a girl to whom he became passionately attached. The case was called at the King's Bench on November 23, 1682, before the Lord Chief Justice assisted by Sir William Dolben, Serjeant Jeffreys, and others. Ford Lord Grey and various accomplices, male and female, were charged with the offence that, on August

20, 1682, at Epsom, where, at Durdans, Lord Berkeley had his home:

'they did falsely, unlawfully, unjustly, and wickedly, by unlawful and impure ways and means, conspire, contrive, practise and intend the final ruin and distruction of Lady Henrietta Berkeley, then a virgin unmarried within the age of eighteen years, daughter, and under the custody of the Rt. Hon. George, Earl of Berkeley'.

The case seemed made out, and the jury had retired to consider their verdict when the following extraordinary dialogue took place, as the result of Grey playing what can only be considered a trump card.

Lord Berkeley : 'My Lord Chief Justice, I desire I may have my daughter delivered to me again.'

Lord Chief Justice : 'My Lord Berkeley must have his daughter again.'

Justice Dolben : 'My Lord, she being now in Court, and there being a writ *De Homo Replegiando* against my Lord Grey for her, upon which he were committed, we must now examine her. Are you under any custody or restraint, Madam?'

Lady Henrietta : 'No, my Lord, I am not.'

Lord Chief Justice : 'Then we cannot deny my Lord Berkeley the custody of his own daughter.'

Lady Henrietta : 'My Lord, I am MARRIED.'

Lord Chief Justice : 'To whom?'

Lady Henrietta : 'To Mr Turner.'

Lord Chief Justice : 'What Turner? Where is he?'

Lady Henrietta : 'He is here in Court.'

Way was made for Mr Turner and he stood by the lady and the Judges.

Lord Chief Justice : 'Let's see him that has married you. Are you married to this lady?'

Mr Turner : 'Yes, my Lord, I am so.'

Lord Chief Justice : 'What are you?'

Mr Turner : 'I am a gentleman.'

Lord Chief Justice : 'Where do you live?'

Mr Turner: 'Sometimes in town, sometimes in the country.'
Lord Chief Justice: 'Where do you live when you are in the country?'
Mr Turner: 'Sometimes in Somerset.'

At this the Justices suggested that Mr Turner might be the son of Sir William Turner.

'He is a little like him,' said Justice Dolben.

Serjeant Jeffreys averred that Mr Turner had been married before and 'thus is all part of the same design and one of the foulest practices that ever was used . . .', which Mr Turner denied.

Questioned by Serjeant Jeffreys about a woman he had lived with as man and wife and had children by her, Mr Turner denied the same, saying: 'My Lord, there is no such thing, but *this* is my wife I acknowledge'.

As a result of Mr. Turner's appearance and intervention, no judgment was entered upon record, in spite of the fact that the jury found Grey and his accomplices guilty of conspiracy. Nor had the unfortunate Berkeleys any consolation, for, as the Countess of Northampton wrote to her sister the Countess of Rutland: 'Gon she is for sartine . . . and left a very distracted house, her pouer mother so afflicted that my sister believes it will kill her'.

It was not long before Grey was in further trouble. He was involved first in a riot and in an assault on the Lord Mayor of London, a matter which cost him a heavy fine, and later as being active in the Rye House Plot, the purpose of which was to assassinate both the King and the Duke of York on their way back from racing at Newmarket. Monmouth was deep in this, and it had been arranged that he was to be concealed at Uppark a week beforehand, 'so that he might not be secured if there was any suspicion . . . '.

The plot failed; executions followed, and Grey and others went into exile or hiding. Grey was actually arrested, but made his guard drunk, and after a series of adventures got away to his home, where he was joined by Lady Henrietta and Mr Turner. The house was unsafe as a refuge, but a ship was waiting for them in Chichester harbour, and the party got away to Flushing without being intercepted. Grey lived at various places abroad till the time of Charles II's death in February 1685, when he hastened to join his fellow exile, Monmouth, in an attempt to secure the throne.

Grey gained little reputation in adversity. Saul Silence, writing to Diana Hayes from Amsterdam, said:

'Lord Grey is a great drinker and brawler hereabouts. An enthusiastic independent fellow who loves gunpowder for the smell of it . . . what he is for I have yet to discover. He lives here with a firm-chinned baggage who reminded me somewhat of you, she has your stubbornness and is easily provoked when teased . . . '

The story of Monmouth's Rebellion is one of ineptitude, with disastrous consequences to the band who joined him. Grey, the only peer to land with Monmouth at Lyme Regis on June 11, 1685, was given charge of the horse, but his conduct at the Battle of Sedgmoor, where the pathetic volunteers who joined the Protestant banner were hopelessly defeated by the soldiers of King James, was inglorious. He fled the field with Monmouth, and was captured on July 7, 1686 by troops under the charge of Lord Lumley, his neighbour at Stanstead. Grey was then not far from Ringwood in the New Forest, Monmouth being taken early next day. Within a week, Monmouth died on the scaffold, while Grey turned King's evidence to save his skin, or in less polite terms, confessed everything he knew, implicating his friends in the process.

Grey' letter of submission to James II was in the following abject terms:

'If the shedding of my blood,' he wrote, 'can be to Your Majesty's interest, I shall be very willing to part with it: and only desire I may have the satisfaction to know that it will be an atonement for the crimes I have committed against you; but if Yr Majesty out of Yr great clemency shall think fit to save me, I hope you will believe that (besides the ties of honour, justice and gratitude) my own inclination will ever oblige me to sacrifice the life you give to your service when you please to command it.

'I lie, Sir, at Your Majesty's feet, where, though I cannot expect, yet it is a pleasure to beg for mercy. The consideration of myself destroys all hopes of that kind, but the observation of your Majesty's universal goodness affords me many. I pray God bless your Majesty with a long and happy reign over your people; and may all those perish that ever lift up a thought against yr Majesty's life or for disturbing the peace of your Government.—Your Majesty's most unfortunate subject.

Ford Grey.'

The letter was dated July 21st, a few days after Monmouth's execution. It was followed by another.

'May it please your Majesty,' wrote Grey, 'Having received Your Majesty's command by my Lord Lumley, that I should in writing acquaint you with all I know of the designed rebellion in Your Majesty's brother's time, the late King; and with the correspondence the late Duke of Monmouth held in England, in order to his rebellion against Your Majesty (in which I was unfortunately engaged and in my heart do sincerely repent of) I have, in obedience to Your Majesty, given you the fullest account I can; and call God to witness (in whose hands I am) that I have not wilfully concealed any thing from you, that I think of the least importance for Your Majesty to know; and this I have done to make the best reparation I can both to God and Your Majesty, for my sin against him in my rebellion against you. Had not the fear of death been an inducement to me, I should have followed the example of those who have made discoveries; but I did not think it became me to treat with Your Majesty, nor to ask that of you which I could have no pretensions to.'

These letters improved Grey's position almost at once. On August 24th he saw his only child, Mary, for the first time since his imprisonment, and on the following day his forgiving wife came to visit him, an order being made out that she should be allowed access whenever she pleased. Grey's brothers and sister were also allowed on visits, and by November he was free.

Grey owed his release partly to his wealth, by means of which he was able to secure the help of Robert Spencer, Earl of Sunderland, one of James's principal officers of State. Sunderland was as unscrupulous as Grey, and a bond of £40,000 was more than adequate to secure his good offices. The enormous bribe, and the fact that Grey was willing to betray his friends, did more than

23

merely save his life. Once free, he was able to trim his sails so well that when, in 1688, William of Orange landed at Torbay with a better favoured expedition than Monmouth's, James looked in vain for Grey to redeem his written promise to shed his blood on his behalf. He wrote from Uppark on November 10, 1688 to his kinsman, Mr Secretary Caryll, in the following terms:

'Cousen

I am extremely obliged to you for the just opinion you have of my Loyalty and zeale for his Majesty's service, and thinke myself verry unfortunate that I am not in a condition to give those proofs of both which my inclinations as well as duty would carry me to FOR I have received lately so violently a fall from my horse (of which Mr Turner will more at large inform you) that tis with great difficulty I now write to you, and that which heightens my misfortune is your assureing me by his Majesties direction that my company and service will be acceptable to him in this expedition; therefore, Sr, as you have been pleased to acquaint the King with your kind thoughts of me, oblige me yet further by communicating to his Majesty the contents of this; and also that I am what he shall ever find me upon all occasions, his Majesty's dutifull and Loyall subject—

I am sr, your most humble servant,
Grey.'

Grey had turned his coat for the last time, and he felt so sure of the favour of the Prince of Orange, soon to reign as William III, that he planned the rebuilding of his Sussex house. His faith in his luck was justified. Within seven years he had become Privy Councillor and Earl of Tankerville, honours which were followed by appointments as Commissioner of Trade, First Commissioner of the Treasury, and finally Lord Privy Seal. Few careers have been less honourable than Grey's, more fortunate —or briefer. He only enjoyed the office of Lord Privy Seal for a year before he died, on June 24, 1701, at his home in Pall Mall. He was forty-seven, and he had crowded a great deal into his life, little of it creditable. No doubt Dryden echoed a general sentiment when he dismissed Grey, in his satire *Absolom and Achitophel*, as 'Cold Caleb' who was 'below the dignity of verse'.

Apart from Uppark, Grey's most extensive memorial, a picture at Chillingham serves to recall its builder. This shows him as a boy, his alert dark eyes already full of mischief. His personality, in the last analysis, is elusive, but a strange glimpse was revealed in 1847, when his coffin was opened in the chancel vault of Harting church. His hand was found to be clasping a Dutch clay pipe. Was it merely indicative of a soothing habit, or was it symbolic of the turn of his luck when a Dutchman ruled at the Court of St. James?

There is no record of the exact years during which the next Uppark was built, but every indication that it was after the newly created Earl of Tankerville had found favour with William III. The architect he employed may possibly have been William Talman, who was Comptroller of the King's Works from 1689 to William III's death in 1702, though evidence is lacking. Talman was employed extensively in alterations under Wren's direction at Hampton Court, and among his extant buildings are Dyrham Park, in Gloucestershire, the south court-yard front of Drayton House, and the south and east fronts of Chatsworth.

One of the first to admire Uppark was Celia Fiennes, who rode by on her way to Chichester, probably in 1695, though the exact date is uncertain. Celia recorded in her rather breathless diary:

'I went to Chichester through a very fine Parke of the Lord Tankervaille's stately woods and shady tall trees at least 2 mile, in the middle stands his house which is new built, square, 9 windows in the front and seven in the sides, brickwork with free stone coynes and windows, itts in the midst of fine gardens, gravell and grass walks and bowling green, with breast walls divideing each from the other and so discovers the whole to view; att the entrance a large Court with iron gates open, which leads to a less, ascending some stepps free stone in a round, thence up more stepps to a terrass, so to the house: it looks very neate and all orchards and yards convenient.'

There is confirmation of Celia Fiennes' observation in a drawing made by Johannes Kip, about the same time as her peregrination. From this it is evident that the main entrance was originally on the east side. There are the two fore-courts, with two sets of iron gates flanked by two stable blocks of identical appearance. In Kip's work the gardens are shown laid out in the rigidly geometrical patterns favoured by the advanced taste of the day, but it is improbable that Tankerville ever carried out anything quite so formal or elaborate as Kip indicates.

Uppark is a type of building whose inspiration derives originally from the Netherlands, other examples being at Ramsbury, Eltham Lodge and Melton Constable. Their style is characterized by a two-storeyed brick construction with simple stone architraves, quoins (Celia's 'coynes') and string-course; a steep-hipped roof; a pronounced cornice, with modillions; and a pediment over the centre of the main front, in the case of Uppark, the south. The tympanum of the pediment is carved with festoons of flowers, and it once carried the Tankerville arms, which have since been replaced by those of Fetherstonhaugh. The general effect is of gravity and repose, seemliness and proportion. It is a style which neither deceives nor declaims. Its virtue is in its grace and calculated simplicity. There is not a trace of vulgarity about it.

Externally, Uppark remains Tankerville's, except for modifications made in the eighteenth and early nineteenth century under the eye of later owners. Inside, alterations have been extensive, but Tankerville's home, with its panels of 'fir wood' painted pink with white mouldings, the great staircase white and gold, must have been exceptionally attractive, judging by the Hall and Dining Room, which retain much of their original decoration. It certainly pleased his successors, for during the half century between the original building and the advent of the Fetherstonhaughs, they were content to let well alone.

In 1695 Tankerville's daughter Mary married Charles Bennett, second Lord Ossulton, at Harting. She brought her husband favour as well as wealth, for the earldom was revived for him in 1714. Charles, Earl of Tankerville in the new creation, died at Uppark eight years after his elevation, and was succeeded by a son of the same name. Both men were prominent in affairs in the north, and became Knights of the Thistle.

Ford Lord Tankerville's grandson Charles reverted to type, in so far as amorous propensities were concerned. He married, probably before he was of age, under romantic circumstances. At an Assize Ball at Newcastle on Tyne he met Camilla Colville, a belle of sixteen. Scenting trouble, the Colville parents shipped the damsel over to Rotterdam, but Ossulton, as the wooer then was, went off in pursuit. According to Longstaffe's *History of Darlington* 'the linden walks of Rotterdam lent their shade to the meetings of the lovers and . . . his lordship made signals from the street, which Camilla could furtively read in the friendly mirror projecting from the parlour window'. Although Camilla was sent back to England, her wooer remained hot in pursuit, for he secreted himself on board the same vessel in a cask. 'The pair landed together at South Shields,' says Longstaffe, 'and shortly afterwards they were married at Jarrow Church, for ages the resort of young couples seeking to enter the bonds of matrimony without the consent of parents.'

It would be pleasant to record that the two lived happily ever after, but that is unlikely, for a letter from Lady Mary Caryll, a kinswoman and neighbour in Sussex, written in September 1738, suggests that Tankerville, as by then he had become, was keeping a lady at Uppark who certainly would not have been received in polite society. This 'madame', as she is described, sent for Tankerville's heir in haste one day, saying that his father had a 'violent fever and convulsions' and seemed about to die. The alarm was premature. Tankerville lived until 1753, when he died of apoplexy, while travelling, at the Green Man, Epping Forest. His wife became Lady of the Bedchamber to Queen Caroline, Consort of George II. Lord Hervey said of her that she was a 'handsome, good natured, simple woman', while Sir Robert Walpole went further, and told the Queen that she was a very safe fool, and 'would give the King some amusement without giving her Majesty any trouble'. Lady Tankerville died in 1775, long after Uppark had passed from the hands of her husband's family.

II

Sir Matthew and
Lady Fetherstonhaugh

The Fetherstonhaughs, like the Greys of Werke, were Northumbrian. A castle bearing their name is extant in Tynedale, where, records a local historian, the stones are stratified 'featherwise'—hence a name admitting of variations from which the terminal 'haugh' is sometimes omitted. In earlier centuries the castle was more picturesque than comfortable. Sir Harry Fetherstonhaugh, to whom in due time Uppark descended, wrote early in the nineteenth century that his ancestors 'poor souls (tho' they were probably as respectable as their contemporaries) knew no more of luxurious agreements than the Laplanders, and I might have been shivering in the old gothic hall at Fetherstone Castle with only a frigid sense of its antiquity'.

Sir Henry Fetherstonhaugh, baronet, through whose will Uppark was bought into the family, was born in 1654, in the same year as Ford, Lord Grey, and was bred to trade. He lived for some years in Spain, and when he returned home married Maria Williamson, the daughter of a London merchant. Sir Henry accumulated a large fortune, certainly not less than £400,000—infinitely more in terms of today—and as neither he nor his nine brothers and sisters had children, he chose as his heir a young kinsman, Matthew Fetherstonhaugh, who, born in 1714, was brought up at Fetherstonhaugh Castle.

Sir Henry died in 1746 at the age of ninety-two, possessed of land in the City of London, Essex, Hertfordshire and Middlesex, in addition to properties in the north country. As the heir's father was wealthy in his own right, and had married an heiress, Matthew Fetherstonhaugh could expect to become in time a still richer man. He had to wait for such superfluity, for his father did not die until 1762, when he had reached the age of ninety-seven.

Two conditions were attached to Sir Henry Fetherstonhaugh's legacy, both of them agreeable. Matthew was to buy himself a baronetcy, which was gazetted on January 3, 1747,[1] and he was to settle in the south. He bought Uppark from Lord Tankerville in 1747, and very soon began to acquire surrounding properties, particularly those of the Carylls, a family which, deeply respected in the district, and having supplied squires of Harting for centuries, was by now in financial difficulties. Uppark cost him £19,000. He had already married Sarah, daughter of Christopher Lethieullier, her family being originally of Brabant, distinguished for business acumen and admirable taste.

Since Uppark's fate was to be alteration and embellishment, it could not have fallen into kinder hands than those of Sir Matthew and his wife. Sarah Fetherstonhaugh already possessed what is one of Uppark's most valuable treasures, a doll's house dating from the 1720s, when she was a child; it is equipped with every appurtenance becoming to a Georgian household.

Standing on an arched pedestal, it is seven feet high, seven feet long and three feet deep. It has nine rooms, the contents of which remain exactly as they were. Footmen in frogged liveries wait in hall or dining room, or lurk on the main stairway with its turned balusters. The housekeeper, in her picot-edged ribbon cap, sits in her room on a wide cane chair, and a nurse, holding one of the family's pallid twins, sits beside the still delicate mother prone in her high four-poster bed.

A silver chandelier hangs above the dining-room table, which is laid with silver plate and tankards. At the back of the room a blue and gold painted alcove, with half moon shelves, holds a silver Queen Anne candlestick and a pair of snuffers in a tray, while on console tables are Waterford glass goblets.

In the drawing room waxen ladies in wide taffeta skirts, and a solitary gentleman, dress-sword at his side, are having a dignified tea party, with a complete silver tea-set on a silver tray with a silver spirit-lamp on a stand. The tiny cups and saucers have silver rat-tail spoons. In the fireplace flowers are embossed on the silver fire-back, and the Lethieullier arms, repeated on the wall sconces, which each have their glass smoke consumers.

All four bedrooms have four-poster beds with their original

---

[1] Some years ago the Deed of Baronetcy was found, along with others, in a brown leather case, resting on the rafters of the housekeeper's store-room.

hangings, blue and rose, cherry and saffron, and all the mirrors are framed in gesso, or bevelled in Vauxhall mirror style. Even the pins, in dresses and table hangings, are hand-made, ageless, rustless.

Among other possessions which also derive from the Lethieullier connection is a series of portraits by Arthur Devis, which hang on the great staircase and are among the best examples of this artist's work. Their subjects are Lethieulliers and their kinsmen the Iremongers. Thanks to the vogue of the conversation-piece and the smaller single portrait, Devis and the best of his contemporaries have been one of the more exciting 'rediscoveries' of the present day, and the choice was undoubtedly Sarah's, since Devis—who was paid fifteen guineas in 1748—included her relations only.

Inside Uppark, the young pair kept the Staircase Hall much as it was in Tankerville's era. Two views, perhaps by Pieter Tillemans, which hang therein, show Uppark as it was, the stables in their original position on the east side, with huntsmen portrayed in the blue and silver livery favoured by the Charlton Hunt.

The Drawing Room reflects mainly eighteenth-century taste, and the white and gold Saloon on the south side of the house— converted out of the marble hall of the Tankervilles—was certainly Matthew and Sarah's creation, to achieve which they had to raise the old level of the first floor, which was a considerable undertaking. In style this Saloon makes the transition from the Palladian to the Adam manner, a fact most clearly seen in the ceiling, where the treatment of the central oval is characteristically Palladian, while the stucco work of the surrounding panels anticipates to some degree the Adam style.

Much of the flock wallpaper introduced by Sir Matthew and Sarah is preserved, and in the Saloon and elsewhere the curtains of French and Italian brocade, with their fringes and pelmets, are original. Door and window fittings are delicately carved and gilded, re-echoing in the Saloon the Adamesque motives in the plaster-work ceiling. The mouldings are of great beauty, and the total effect is a white and gold room of extreme refinement, an appropriate setting for the portraits by Nathaniel Dance of George III and Queen Charlotte in coronation robes, believed to have been shown at the first Royal Academy.

The decoration of the Little Parlour was left much as it was, though it was partly refurnished, and what is now known as the Stone Hall, but what was then the Entrance Hall, was also not much altered, nor was the Dining Room. From the adjoining Serving Room a staircase led to a basement whence a door opened into underground passages built later by Sir Matthew to connect with the kitchens, larders, laundry and stables, all of which were in outbuildings, at first to the east and later to the north of the house. When these old kitchen quarters were in use, food was carried through the passages on wooden trolleys fitted with charcoal heaters, while in the Serving Room itself further hot plates were provided. This was a cumbersome procedure, time and heat-wasting. It entailed the employment of a large kitchen staff, who would certainly have eaten their own food hotter than that of the family and their guests. The system survived for two centuries. Sir Matthew and his lady made a tour of the Continent between 1749 and 1751, during which time they missed no chance of adding objects of art to their collection, not only for Uppark, but for a London home planned and shortly to be built by James Paine in Whitehall. Once known as Dover House, this occupied the site of what is now the Scottish Office, and the estimate came to £5,894 0s 5½d! The pair were painted in Venice by Rosalba Carriera the pastelist, and in Rome by Pompeo Battoni, works which remain in their home.

Like many rich men, Sir Matthew was meticulous in keeping accounts, and as many books of these have been preserved, neatly written in his own hand, it is possible to estimate his expenditure in the years following his advent to Uppark. In the first year alone the total was in the neighbourhood of £100,000, much of the outlay being land purchase (he was an avid buyer of local property), furnishings and building operations. So far as building was concerned, the work was always carried out under the management of Miller, a trusted foreman. Sir Matthew was a sociable man, not at all averse to gambling in neighbouring houses such as Goodwood, Petworth and Charlton, and his losses and gains were duly noted.

At Buriton not far away lived Gibbon, father of the author of *The Decline and Fall of the Roman Empire*, and that the Gibbons and Fetherstonhaughs were on close terms is proved by a reference in Edward Gibbon's correspondence following a visit to Trajan's Column. 'Figure to yourself a Column 140 foot high of the purest white marble,' wrote the historian, 'composed only of about 30 blocks and wrought into bas-reliefs with as much taste and delicacy as any chimneypiece at Up-park.'

Typical entries in Fetherstonhaugh accounts for the year 1746 run as follows:

'For pistols: £11.11. Dancing Master £2.2.
Journey to Uppark exclusive of Turnpike £3.2.5.
For Satin for a waistcoat £3.1.0.
For a bag and wig £1.16.6. Gave a poor man £1.1.0.
For worsted lace £5.0.0. For a telescope 21/-
For a nosegay 1/-. A cane 5/-
Ruffles and muslin £12.15s.0.
For French Horns £6.8.0. Chocolate £2.15.0. Play 7/6
Chair 5/-.
At Ye Coffe House and Rooms 12/-. Booksellers 5/-. Musik 5/-.
At Goodwood 7/1. For a hat 9/1.
In 1754 Dresden China 11/- and again for the same £39.10.'

Some of the above entries reveal a charming sense of what was fitting—for instance the items to make a gay appearance at the Play.

Sir Matthew sometimes argued against the extravagancies of his mode of life, comparing rather ruefully the expense of living in London as against Uppark, and entered in particular detail the cost of his coaches and horses, his men, food and keep.

'Suppose,' he wrote, 'I stay 30 weeks in the Country the Difference of keeping my Horses there and in Town will be £38 only which deducted from £294.0.0.

38.
———————

£256 remnant.
With sum of £256 my seven horses stand me in at least exclusive and the 3 Serv^{ts} diet; and travelling charges, as well as Candles and some other trifles, and exclusive of Stabling both in Town and Country which I find in the above Calculation.'

At the foot of this page of 'Calculations' he added:

'The Difference between hiring and keeping yr own, I suppose you always keep 7 Horses and live 30 weeks in the Country, the diet of the Serv^ts will be equal.'

This is exactly the sort of note to be found in most private account books—plain to the writer, for whose sole eye it was intended—not so easy to follow for a reader who lights upon it in a later age.

Under the items of coaches and saddlery, purchase of horses, hide of chairs and coaches, corn and fodder, Sir Matthew spent £936 in six months. In the same period he spent on:

'Wigs and apparel:	£210
Furnishings:	535
Clocks and watches:	128
Plate:	115
Jewelry:	47
Pictures:	262
	———
Totalling £1,297'	

Sir Matthew entered the following interesting facts about his Continental tour and the monies he expended on Uppark during his absence. In 1748 he estimated that he expended abroad 'from the time I left England until I return all £700' on travelling.

Later, he entered:

'About this time went abroad till Sept 29 1751. Last year 1752, £5,500. Building from the above time to Jan. 1753: £3,000.

Before I went abroad:	£7,500	(Before 1749)	
To 1753	:	3,000	Uppark besides
To 1756	:	4,000	furniture
	———		
	£15,000	(*sic*)	

He added cautiously:

'It may be £300 or £400 more but this I am certain of.'

Again:

'By another account extracted from Miller's books and my own, it (all) amounts to £16,615.15/-, up to Jan. 1st 1759.'

These sums did not include his enormous expenditure on other details of life in London and in the country.

Sir Matthew embarked on plans for planting, spending £13 15s 6d on chestnuts and fir trees. It may have been at this date that the existing Scots firs were planted. He paid £5 5s od for red deer and £49 on the park palings. Lady Fetherstonhaugh asked him for orange trees and myrtles, which were admired by Mr Repton, the landscape gardener, when he came to Uppark in 1811. 'Charges on the pond . . . £9.1.4d.', may have been for the water supply, or for the pond in front of the house.

'A piece of chints' cost £210. There still are interesting 'pieces of chints' of every age carefully preserved at Uppark. Fifteen guineas were paid for a watch and £4 for forty brace of carp. Another item of interest is: '£123.7.2d. paid for window sashes' in 1748. The tinted glass of the astragal windows still remains. Some china cups cost £5 15s 6d.

Sir Matthew was a man of ranging interests and alert intelligence, with an excellent working library which included works by Clarendon, Locke, Addison, Bolingbroke, and Samuel Johnson. Like Pepys, he learnt and used a form of shorthand, a practice with which he enthused his wife. He had a delicate pocket microscope for the study of natural objects, and he actually committed his reflections on 'Natural Philosophy' to paper, the idea of Matter and Form, particularly that of Natural Bodies, engaging his attention.

Form arising from 'different texture' and 'distinctive essence' caused him to note that:

'The Forms of Bodies are nothing but this different Texture, arising from the Motion, Magnitude and Figure of the minute particles of Matter: and in this consists the internal Constitution and real Essence of every Species of Bodies.'

With modesty he added:

'As our faculties are not suitable to the Discovery of this, we are fain to distinguish each Species by the Effects of its Form upon our Senses by that Collection of sensible Qualities or Properties, which arise (we know not how) from ye peculiar Texture of its parts . . . '

He filled his manuscript books with cautious conclusions, 'in ye Principles of Natural Philosophy', carefully adding 'as it now stands'. 'Hypotheses are not to be relied on,' he decided, 'but must give way to Experiment, and Observation, from which alone we are enabled to pronounce anything with assurance concerning natural bodies.'

'Conclusions formed in this Manner (Which is called the Method of Analysis) will not admit of any but what Experience and Observation have confirmed.'

But, he affirmed:

'The matter of which the world consists was at first put in motion by the Creator, and afterwards left to itself to produce all the heavenly Bodies by Means of that Motion. . . '

Sir Matthew was a Fellow of the Royal Society, which in his day readily admitted amateurs of science, and among his more advanced experiments were some concerned with electricity, which he defined as 'a Power in Bodies, whereby they attract and repel light Bodies at a considerable Distance'.

Purple flame and snapping noises diverted him. Experiments with a glass bowl and a gun-barrel seem to have caused him and his friends considerable entertainment. There is a certain charm in thinking of this circle of brocade-coated gentlemen gathered round a shot-gun which hung by silken cords near a glass globe, while a wheel and a wooden frame was whirled by hand and, in the words of Sir Matthew:

'whether this has received the Quantity of Electricity sufficient to make experiment, may be shown by holding the finger to the barrel, when it will be much electrified, cause a sense of Numbness and Pricking and flashes of purple flame will start with a snapping Noise both from the gun-barrel and your Finger . . . '

Other less carefully bound little books of white calf contain Sir Matthew's essays in Philosophic thought and Science generally. They helped to make up his private world. In a public way, his wealth enabled him to take a considerable part in affairs.

He had big interests in East India Stock (about £16,000) and Bank of England Stock; he was an early supporter of the building of new canals; and he was a Governor of St. Thomas's and the Middlesex Hospitals; but before still wider fields engrossed him, he and Sarah were gladdened first by the birth of an heir, their only child, and then by the election of Sir Matthew to Parliament.

A paper in Sarah Fetherstonhaugh's writing, preserved in the house, tells much in few words:

'Sir Harry Fetherstonhaugh was born at Uppark on December 22nd 1754 at half an hour past ten in the morning; he was innoculated March 24th 1758; and had the measles in March 1770.'

A proud father had already prepared himself for the event as well as such a progressive man could. In 1753, for the sum of sixpence, he had acquired *An Essay Upon Nursing, and the Management of Children; from their Birth to three years of Age.* This was by William Cadogan, M.D. (LEYDEN AND OXFORD), B.A., an army doctor who practised later at Bristol and later still at the Foundling Hospital in Brunswick Square.

In this book, bound with a leather back and marbled boards, Sir Matthew inscribed his name on the fly-leaf. Parents were enjoined by the author to adopt a new outlook, particularly in the matter of diet. Dr Cadogan deplored the habit of giving the wrong food to the infant:

'The general Practice is, as soon as a Child is born, to cram a Dab of Butter and Sugar down its throat, a little Oil, Panada, Caudle, or some such unwholesome Mess. So that they set out wrong, and the Child stands a fair chance of being made sick from the first hour. It is the custom of some to give a little roast Pig to an Infant; which, it seems, is to cure it of all Mother's Longings. I wish these Matters were a little more enquired into,' adds the worthy Doctor, 'for the Honour of the Sex . . . '

He stressed the fact that, 'The Feeding of Children properly is of much greater importance to them than their Cloathing . . . '; but he gave most modern advice about their garments:

' . . . laying aside all those Swathes, Bandages, Stays, and Contrivances, that are most ridiculously used to close and keep the Head in its Place and support the Body. As if Nature, exact Nature, had produced her chief Work, a human Creature, so carelessly unfinished as to want those Idle Aids to make it perfect. Shoes and Stockings are very needless Incumbrances, besides that they keep the Legs wet and nasty . . . a child would stand firmer and learn to walk much sooner without them . . . '

Nurses were engaged and supported; Mrs Alcorn, at the head of this department, had a position of great responsibility in the household and it is reasonably certain that no roast pig passed infant lips. Almost the first reference to Harry in the account book was for his 'buttons' in March 1758: they cost £1 11s 6d. Later, in 1761, 3s was paid for his gloves, and in April of that year, he had his hair cut at a charge of 5s. In October of the same year, he was given a magnificent present, a watch, for which his father paid fifteen guineas, with an additional 7s 6d for a chain and key. In the same year, in March, is an item 'Harry's horse £1.15.0d'. This was also the time when one guinea was paid for a writing master for his instruction, the first of many payments for his education while he prepared for Eton.

The old nurse, no doubt chosen with much care, as being open to the most up-to-date advice, must have held a favoured position throughout her life. She was mentioned in Sir Matthew's will, and given security for life. She and the baby may well have been installed in the room which was always particularly Sir Harry's, on the east side of the house, with access to the old back stairs. His mother's was nearby, separated from the stairs by red baize doors.

The matter of Harry's early education was entrusted locally. The living of Harting was, until 1949, a sinecure Rectorship, with a vicar appointed by the Rector. In later years, the Rector generally appointed himself, but in Harry's childhood the vicarage was occupied by a Dr Durnford, whose daughter had married Ulrick Fetherstonhaugh, Sir Matthew's clerical brother, who succeeded to the Rectorship in 1757. It was Ulrick and his wife with whom Sir Matthew and his lady had been on the Continent, and a portrait of Mrs Ulrick by Battoni which hangs in the Little Drawing Room suggests what a charming companion she must have been.

Dr Durnford, the Vicar, was learned and charming, and he possessed a lovely handwriting which was a model for his pupil. Harry's earliest exercise showed confidence and promise. His copybooks are models of propriety and careful spelling, of neatness and punctiliousness, serving to equip him for Eton and University College, Oxford, where he matriculated in 1772, at the age of eighteen.

The matter of Sir Matthew's entry into Parliament, though it could indeed be arranged, was not quite so simple as engaging nurses and following Dr Cadogan's advice with regard to the child. Sir Matthew was a Whig, an adherent of the party managed by the Duke of Newcastle and his brother, Henry Pelham.

In 1754 he stood for Parliament at Andover, where his step brother-in-law, Joshua Iremonger, had considerable interest. Matthew had Newcastle's support, and 'was going to see what his friends can do for him'. But he failed to get in, and he asked Newcastle if he could succeed William Hay at Seaford in 1755. On being told that the seat was promised to James Peachey, he was piqued, and when Newcastle informed him, through John Page, of an unexpected vacancy at Tiverton, where 'there can be no doubt of success with very little expense', Sir Matthew did not relish the idea. But on Robert Ord being appointed Chief Baron of the Exchequer in Scotland, Newcastle suggested that Sir Matthew should succeed him at Morpeth.

With his Northumbrian ancestry and upbringing in mind, Sir Matthew replied that ' . . . nothing could be more satisfactory than serving for one in Northumberland'. But he objected to paying more than £500 or £600, and wished to avoid a journey to the north, or else that the expense should be included in the sum. Newcastle replied that the expense would be not more than £600 and that 'you need not give yourself the trouble of a journey'. Sir Matthew was returned unopposed on November 29, 1755.

In 1759, he was offered a seat in Essex by a group of leading Essex Whigs but he declined standing, or undertaking to stand at the next general election.

In October one of Lord Carlisle's Executors wrote to the Duke of Newcastle that at Morpeth some Yorkshire Militia officers had offered 'money for the choosing of a Member the next election'. Newcastle, much surprised, forwarded the letter to Sir Matthew, but did not feel able to oppose the Carlisle interest in the matter of the Morpeth election; however, he assured his friend of a seat in the next Parliament. Sir Matthew replied that he had had previous warning 'of the secret contrivances for this change'. The Carlisle manager had told a friend of his that he could not be elected again.

Newcastle kept his promise, and on his recommendation to Lord Anson, Sir Matthew Fetherstonhaugh was returned, with Admiralty support, for Portsmouth in 1761. He kept this seat until his death in 1774. On March 12, 1761, J. Cleveland wrote to the Duke of Newcastle:

'I have taken the very first opportunity of communicating to my Lord Anson your Grace's inclinations to have Sir Matthew Fetherston recommended to Portsmouth, which I find is very agreeable to his Lordship and he will be recommended with Sir Edward Hawke accordingly.'

On April 1, 1761, Sir Matthew wrote to Newcastle thanking him:

' . . . for having recommended me to so worthy a set of Gentlemen as this Corporation seems to consist of; for everything was done with great order and decency; and after the Election was over we finished the Evg. with great mirth and jollity.'

He was already a very busy man, but this did not prevent him from adding the cares and interests of a growing constituency to his daily occupations. Sir Matthew kept Newcastle informed of the news of troubles among the seamen, and first news of dockyard strikes was brought to Uppark.

On May 13, 1768, he wrote to the Duke:

'The seamen are more turbulent I hear today, and threaten fire to the shipping. All the labourers I hear now are to meet tomorrow for to agree upon methods to get an addition of wages . . . '

Sir Matthew received his Parliamentary Whip direct from Newcastle both in October 1761 and 1762; he was classed in Bute's Parliamentary List of December 1761 as 'Newcastle'.

By the autumn of 1763 he was classed as 'Conservative'; not then a party designation, but an indication that he was 'safe'. Under the Government of Lord Grenville he voted steadily in Opposition; and he was always counted by Newcastle among his 'sure friends . . . to be sent to upon any occasion'.

He voted with the Opposition on the Land Tax in February 1767; over payment of the King's Debts in 1769; in the Divisions over Wilkes in the Middlesex Election, and the Spanish Convention of 1771. In the year following he is noted as 'Conservative, sick, present'; but he did not vote on March 11, 1772. He does not appear to have voted in any subsequent divisions.

The Duke of Richmond wrote to Edmund Burke on December 2, 1772:

'I . . . went to Uppark to my friend Sir Matthew Fetherstonhaugh . . . I found that all idea of getting him to London was in vain. He has been in a very dangerous illness for several months. He is now better . . . but feels, and with great reason, that if he was to venture out . . . it might cost him his life.'

There is no record of Sir Matthew Fetherstonhaugh having spoken in the House, and of his Parliamentary career it may be said that he was a typical Country Member of his time, willing to vote and to serve as the Party Managers to whom he had given his allegiance thought best. As a magistrate, on the other hand, he showed zeal and not a little courage. In an age and in a district held in thrall by the smuggling fraternity, Sir Matthew was fearless on the Bench, in strong contrast to some of his neighbours. It was here, perhaps, that his Northumbrian blood told most. He came from a county where lawlessness was understood and where those in authority needed — and generally acquired — the courage to convict.

Towards the end of his life, Sir Matthew Fetherstonhaugh was drawn into a scheme of land speculation on the ever-moving Western frontier of British America. In 1768 a great Red Indian Conference had been held at Fort Stanwix, to which most of the Indian representatives had come, fiercely determined to resist the depredations of the white settlers on their land west of the Alleghany Mountains. When they met, however, it was to learn that the Iroquois, the most powerful of the tribes, had agreed to accept the sum of £10,000 in compensation for their hunting grounds in a wide area stretching as far as Kentucky. The only Indians not to suffer from this arrangement were the Iroquois themselves, but their neighbours knew that it was useless to oppose them.

A company, to be known as the Grand Ohio Company, was

formed in 1769 to finance the settlement of a colony in the newly released lands which was to be called Vandalia. This Company represented many trading and colonial interests in the states of Virginia and Pennsylvania. One of the American sponsors of the plan was a Mr Samuel Wharton of Philadelphia. He came to England to negotiate with the Government, on behalf of traders, for a more generous attitude towards land grants. He was a leading member of a firm formed for the settlement of new land, and had been present at the dramatic conference at Fort Stanwix.

Between the years 1769 and 1774, Mr Wharton became very well known at Uppark. He sought to petition the Government on behalf of the Grand Ohio Company, to develop a new colony on established lines. Land was already being seized without legality and the predatory habits of immigrants were deplored. Mr Wharton came to voice the opinion of well-established Americans, and, by enthusiastic descriptions of the territory, to enlist the support of influential people in his project. Benjamin Franklin was among the petitioners, and George Washington was privately interested in the outcome of their efforts. The object was to establish peace and security for recognized settlers, and the hope was that for an outlay of about £10,000, for land in what is now West Virginia, property could be acquired which could be resold at a profit of about half a million. The stakes were in fact so high that they account for the extraordinary patience and doggedness shown by Mr Wharton over a long time.

Samuel Wharton's papers at Uppark formed a considerable collection; and in his correspondence he gave Sir Matthew every detail of his dealings with Cabinet Ministers and others in authority in London.

A certain Dr Arthur Lee and his associates had petitioned in December 1768 for an established Government for the proposed new Colony. A memorandum written by Wharton, to be sent to Lord Hillsborough, pleads that he is 'still at a loss to express any surprise at an event which delays for an unlimited time business that has been so long before your Lordship, which you was pleased to think of much importance and which, by our agreement with the Treasury upon it, has received no small encouragement'.

In forwarding material to Sir Matthew, Mr Wharton empha-
sized that as far back as the year 1748 the Board of Trade had
reported in favour of settlements to the westward of the
Alleghany Mountains, and he pointed out that Lord Halifax
was 'one of those who signed the Report which he now
obstructed'. He enclosed a comprehensive treatise on the whole
situation, and mentioned the names of Lords Camden, Dartmouth, Hillsborough, Hertford, Falmouth, Rochford, North,
Sandwich, Suffolk and the Duke of Grafton, as having been
interested.

On June 16, 1770, Thomas Walpole wrote to the Earl of
Hillsborough as follows:

'My Lord,
   I did Myself the Honor to wait on your Lordship on Wednesday Ye 6th instant with a Paper which I left at Your Lordship's
drawn up by Mr Wharton in favour of the settlement of Land
under a distinct Government on the River Ohio in America.'

Negotiations were tedious and protracted, and in writing to Sir
Matthew on July 24, 1770, Mr Wharton complained of the

'Unfortunate procrastination for me, as I am absent from my
Family and at great Expense. If I continue here to prosecute this
Business to an Issue for the emolument of so many wealthy
partners, may I be permitted to ask whether it is not reasonable
They should at least defray the Expenses I have been and may
be at? . . . '

A year later, in July 1771, Mr Wharton, writing again to Sir
Matthew, told him that:

'almost all the Lords are out of Town, Lord Rochford called a
Cabinet on Thursday night and our affair was again talked over.
Lord Hillsborough then threw off the mask and openly opposed
us, by alledging the bad policy of suffering settlements over the
Mountains, and that the Lands we had agreed for would sell for
£500,000 odd if divided into small parcels etc.'

In the same month he wrote that Lord Rochford 'has manifested
more spirit . . . than all the other Lords except the president
. . . that he will undertake to rouse the other Lords and make
them as active as himself'.

In November 1771 Mr Wharton thanked Sir Matthew very sincerely for 'his kindnesses and civilities at Uppark', but a week or two later added that Lord Hillsborough 'continues obstinately inflexible' and that he was amazed at 'Lord Hillsborough's resolute obstinacy'. On December 14th, Wharton was very grateful to Sir Matthew for 'his most acceptable present of a Doe . . . '. He asked a share of a haunch, to present to some of 'my American friends who are lately arrived'.

Presents, invitations and compliments passed between Wharton and his American associates and the Fetherstonhaughs, and on August 20, 1772, Wharton wrote:

'I do myself the pleasure of informing you that on the 14th instant His Majesty in Council was pleased to approve of and order to be carried into execution the Report of the Committee of the Privy Council in favour of the Grant of Lands to Mr Walpole and his associates, and that a new Government should be established thereon. Mr Walpole proposed calling a General Meeting of the Company to communicate this agreeable news to them.'

He gave an extract of a letter from a gentleman in Philadelphia, who wrote:

' . . . a Joy inconceivably great, as the Grant blessed with a separate Government, is, Incontestably the most valuable obtained of the Crown, Since that made to Mr Penn.'
The writer continued:

' . . . Above 2,300 have arrived from Ireland; of which at least 2,000 paid their passages and are now seeking settlements. It is notorious that twice as many are expected this fall from the same Kingdom, and I have it on good authority that not less than 7,000 Dutch will be imported within two months.'

But while Americans were filled with expectation, the Government delayed, and in 1772 Wharton commented:

'I will not relax in my application, as I am sure by Perseverance I shall conquer him. Lord Dartmouth is gone to Yorkshire and is not expected in Town until the beginning of next month. Lord Suffolk is ill with the gout; and Lord Rochford only comes hither on Wednesdays and returns home on Fridays. It is uncertain when Parliament will meet, and of course as uncertain when the Administrator will be in London to do any kind of Business.

'Happy Country? To be so well established and regulated as that it will sustain its connections and Dependencies without the superintendence of its Rulers? But how much longer will it do well in this way?'

Sir Matthew threw his weight into the endeavours of Mr Wharton to get a fair hearing and satisfaction to his petitions, but the Cabinet remained evasive and obstructive.

In November 1772, Wharton wrote encouraging descriptions of conversations with Cabinet Ministers, and stated that 'Every Wednesday Mr Walpole (his intermediary) is to dine with me in Argyle Street'. He added: 'I think your fears are too great in respect of what Parliament may say or do in our affair. Its administration is determined to complete the job.' Wharton wrote on December 23, 1772:

'I have the pleasure to tell you, that I was this day introduced by Mr Walpole and Mr Pitt to the Earl of D. (Dartmouth) and was received in a very kind Manner by his Lordship. We delivered Him the Clauses for the Grant, and our plan of Government; and it fell to my lot, to explain them particularly: which, to my surprise, consumed an hour and a half.'

Meanwhile, in the same year, he had persuaded Sir Matthew to subscribe £2,105 in a venture to sell merchandise (French match-coating, blue Duffields, Irish and Scotch linens) in Virginia, and his son, Sir Harry, followed in a similar venture (July 1774) to the extent of £447. The accounts do not show that any return was ever received, but the bills of lading remained at Uppark.

Similarly with the Ohio Company, Sir Matthew subscribed £2,000 for half of one share, and in the next year, 1773, paid Major Trent £3,000 for his half share, besides £200 towards the expenses of the Company.

Mr Wharton wrote later, in great excitement, about a conversation with Lord Dartmouth, 'who was found to be perfectly convinced of the propriety of our Grant'.

On July 3, 1773, he reported:

'I have the pleasure to tell good Lady F. from Lord Rochford that her grapes were much admired by the King, but that His Majesty not only expressed his thanks for them, but for the Bucks. I am assured also that he was greatly pleased with the excursion to Portsmouth and with the manoeuvres of the Fleet . . . '

Mr Wharton talked of 'young Harry' as an 'amiable, sweet-tempered, sensible young gentleman', and congratulated his parents 'on the credit which your son acquired at Oxford'. But in the same month, he wrote in despair that,

' . . . In truth—our patience is quite exhausted; and I know so much (acquired at enormous expense of health and money) of them all, and of the manner of completing all business in this venial and corrupt country . . . that no consideration shall, I fear, induce me ever to return to it After I have once revisited America . . . The East India Directors have at last agreed to ship Teas to Philadelphia, New York, etc., but they do it with an ill grace and in an illiberal and pitiful manner . . . '

Throughout, Sir Matthew had shown a clearer appreciation of the situation than the optimistic Mr Wharton. His acquaintance with government made him view the whole situation with caution. He had used the weight of his influence to further the project, but with American unrest against British rule increasing, the politicians thought it wise not to encourage an expansion from which they might never benefit.

The Vandalia venture in fact came to an abrupt end with the American Revolution and the war with the mother country which began in 1775. The letters conclude with one from Thomas Walpole (February 1777) to Sir Harry to say that Mr Wharton 'apprehends that he can be of no use in the further application to Government for lands on the River Ohio, and has therefore closed his account'.

Throughout his fruitless sojourn in England, Mr Wharton complained of ill-health. In October 1772, he looked forward to coming to Uppark and finding Sir Matthew greatly benefited by the medicine 'that you were lately in use of', hoping that the gout and fever had left him. He mentioned Lady Fetherston-haugh and her son having delightful weather for their hunting, and added: 'You and I must content ourselves with the fireside and chatting over the rise of operations of the future rich Colony of Ohio'. But a bilious attack prevented his visit. He bewailed that 'wine and rich viands are prejudicial to me. My driɩk should be toast and water and my dinners the simplest the cook can prepare.'

Sir Matthew's own health had been failing for some time and gave cause for great anxiety. On June 10, 1772, his friend and neighbour, Edward Gibbon the historian, wrote to his sister to tell her that 'Sir Matthew is breaking up very fast', but for two years longer Sir Matthew pursued his interests in the new American Colony.

As soon as he had invested money in Wharton's project, Sir Matthew chose Henry Keene to erect a Gothic tower on the highest point of the Downs in Uppark property, as a fitting memorial to the Vandalian venture.

This Gothic tower stands on a site that can be seen from far and wide, the place chosen being to the north of the house. A little compass drawing among the papers of the period shows with what meticulous care Sir Matthew planned for views over Sussex, Surrey and Hampshire and across the sea to the Isle of Wight.

The Vandalian Tower was built of brick with stone Gothic pinnacles. A kitchen was provided on the ground floor, with a commodious fireplace where the largest joints could be cooked. In an upper room, windows commanded extensive views to north, south and west. Here the company could enjoy the distant prospects, while discussing the talents of the Uppark cooks. In Regency days the feasts were on such a gargantuan scale that it was said that diners had to be trundled down the slopes in wheelbarrows back to the house to sleep.

Sir Matthew did not live to see the fruition of his building plans. He made his will on his deathbed, on March 19, 1774. His directions were:

'That he be buried at Stanford-le-Hope where Sir Henry Fether-stone is buried. That his funeral be private. That Lady Fetherstone's Jointure be punctually paid and £200 p.a. added to it and £3,000 paid her to be at her free disposal.

'That Lady Fetherstone and Benjn Lethieullier her brother

have the care of his only son Henry Fetherstone till he comes to
the age of twenty one years and that his said son be his sole
heir and residuary legatee. That £5,200 be given to the said
Benjamin Lethieullier for the guardianship of his son and £100
more for mourning. That £100 be given to Joshua Iremonger
and £50 for mourning. That £50 be given to his brothers and
sisters for mourning and the same sum to Lascelles Iremonger.
That one hundred pounds per ann be paid his brothers Robert
and Ulrick Fetherstone during their natural lives.

'That a year's wages be paid all his servants over and above
what may be due to them at his death. That the lease of his
Town house be renewed and then sold. That £60 per ann be
paid Sarah Webb during her life. That £100 per ann be paid the
Rev. Mr Dalton till he is better provided for.

The mark of Sir Matthew Fetherstone

signed this 19th March 1774 in the presence of
                            Thos Moore, Edward Pyke, H. Lascelles

This Memorandum Registered at the Court of Canterbury at
London, on the 28th March 1774.

The Registrars require the testamentary Guardians to make 'a
true and perfect Inventory of all and singular the said Goods,
Chattels and Credits and Exhibit the same in six months' time.'

The grief of Sir Harry at the death of his father is shown in a
letter written to a family friend and local magistrate, William
Battine of East Marden, on March 24, 1774:

'After the late melancholy event and the loss of so ever dear a
parent, you will not expect the tender heart of a son to dwell
long upon a subject of so affecting a nature; indeed my spirits
are not calculated for taking pen in hand, did I not think it
incumbent upon me to acknowledge to you the great regard and
gratitude of our worthy friends at Portsmouth who are pleased
to testify it by a generous offer to Mr Iremonger requesting him
to represent that Borough till such time as I am of age . . . '

III

Sir Harry Fetherstonhaugh
in Earlier Life

At the time of his father's death, Sir Harry Fetherstonháugh, who was in Italy on the Grand Tour with his uncle, the Rev. Ulrick Fetherstonhaugh, was in a situation at once enviable and dangerous. His education was almost complete; he was wealthy, and an only son, and a prospect of pleasure or, if he preferred it, of public service in which the duties need not be too onerous, was before him. He had no serious emotional attachments, and his mother was not only alive and most affectionate, but she was prepared to look after his interests, financial and otherwise, with the skill with which she had always conducted her own affairs.

One of the earliest to speculate upon the future of Uppark and its new owner was Edward Gibbon. He was then a man approaching forty who had settled in London, entered the House of Commons as a silent member for Liskeard, and was already in the throes of composition of the earlier volumes of his history. After a visit to Uppark, with which he was already so familiar, he reported:

'At present everything carries the appearance of sobriety and economy. The Baronet . . . returns to his College at Oxford, and even the house at Whitehall is to be let.'

But on January 31, 1775, after another visit, he wrote:

'Sir Harry is very civil and good humoured. But from the unavoidable temper of youth, I fear he will cost many a tear to Lady F. She consults everybody, but has neither authority nor plan.'

It appeared that Sir Harry possessed sensitivity without common sense, and that he had already run into some trouble.

Departure for the Grand Tour had been hastened, so tradition maintains, by a love affair with a local miller's daughter. During the time that Sir Harry was on the Continent with his uncle, his mother was left to find a year's wages for twenty-eight indoor and fifteen outdoor servants which had been bequeathed to them by their late master, and to wrestle with some very complicated accounts.

Possessing the business acumen and methodical habits of her family, she continued in her late husband's admirable habits of bookkeeping. Although her assets were considerable, she was faced with a debt of £18,602 on the estate, and with outstanding legal expenses which were called for by her lawyer, Mr Carleton. One of the earliest decisions to which she was a party was to sell land in Essex and elsewhere. She also sold property in the City of London which included a curiosity shop and two houses in Crooked Lane. East India Stock and timber were also realized, though the proceeds, £37,255, left a balance of only £138 18s 6d over her current expenditure.

Among Lady Fetherstonhaugh's expenses resulting from the death of Sir Matthew were:

Legacies	£1,178	0	0
Wages and mourning	257	0	0
Bills left by Sir Matthew	1,691	0	0
Mr Wharton	447	0	0
Portsmouth claims	2,325	0	0
Total	£5,898	0	0

while his relations were paid over £6,000.

The expense account relating to Sir Harry's Continental tour shows that he took £200 with him in cash. Payments for him at Geneva amounted to over £700; at Rome he spent £600; at Florence he spent £500; at Venice and on his second visit to Rome he was more economical and spent only £200 in each place, and later the same amount in Paris.

His portrait, painted by Pompeo Battoni in Rome in 1776, which now hangs in the Red Drawing Room, shows a rather thin-faced, long-nosed youth with sandy hair. Thirty-six years later Sir Harry wrote from Uppark to Sir Arthur Paget:

'I never suffered so much cold as I did in the winter I passed in Italy because no means are ever thought to provide against such a season. I feel much more obliged to Inigo Jones who built this house . . . '

Sir Harry's observation about Inigo Jones shows that he, at least, had inherited no tradition that his home had been designed by Talman. Although Inigo Jones had been dead some forty years at the time Uppark was created, it is not without his influence.

On his return from his spell abroad, during which time the young man acquired an interest in French taste and literature which lasted him his lifetime, Sir Harry was sensibly content that his mother should manage the economy of his household and in particular his living expenses. A regular item noted in her hand in the account books is:

'to Lady F. ¼ for Sir Harry's Board £100 . . . '

She lived on at Uppark, apart from frequent visits to her Iremonger relations, for the rest of her life, no doubt to their marked benefit. One of her entries shows that her son had accumulated bills at Oxford to the tune of £310 and that the total of all the 'draughts while abroad' came to £2,930.

Typical notes of running expenditure were as follows:

The labour for mowing the parks, and sundries:	£81	17	4
She bought 25 quarters of beans for the deer:	39	0	0
The servants wages came to:	101	0	0
The cost of their clothes:	56	0	0

About fifty men came up from the Harting district each day to work at Uppark. Most of them lived in cottages where they kept a pig, poultry, and where they made their own bread. Sixteen woodmen in round white smocks and tall black hats worked in the beech-woods, and maintained the deer park fences of hand-cleaved oak, to keep in 800 deer which roamed over 900 acres. A deerkeeper lived in a cottage in a pretty dell in the park forest, and he divided venison appropriately among the estate workers. Dewponds provided water in many places. Thousands of sheep fed on the emerald downs and were attended by shepherds in traditional smocks and round black hats, and with shepherds' crooks, who kept careful watch and folded their flocks at night. They told the time by the sun and the stars, and they said, 'Them that sleep o'bed of nights doan't know the smell o' 'oneysuckle . . . '.

Strong teams of horses and sturdy carters marched by the painted haywains and the timber waggons, or beside the teams with high saddle bells that drew the Uppark corn musically, for all to hear, to Chichester. The blacksmiths in the Home Farm forge drank eight pints of the home brewed beer before breakfast, and any of the men could sit in the Old Hall to drink the beer that came in pipes from the Brew House in the stable yard. The grooms ate bread and cheese in the Harness Room, placed on clean stable cloths on the floor. Sir Harry paid for their red and white striped jackets, and for the annual sports, when the women put on long frilled cotton trousers, and when the tug of war was pulled over the Dog Kennel Pond, to ensure that the losers had a ducking.

By the year 1778, Sir Harry's habits and extravagance were beginning to cause anxiety. He was then of an age to enjoy his fortune unhindered; he had no occupation beyond the pursuit of pleasure, and a pathetic note by Lady Fetherstonhaugh, written when drafts on Drummonds Bank amounted to £3,234 within a few months, was the result of sad reflection.

'This year's account Lady F. cannot properly settle, nor carry the balance forward, not knowing what is in the Banker's hands, nor the sums drawn for Sir Harry since Sept 11th 1778, the last time Sir Harry gave me any account . . . '

Soon there was a still greater trial: Sir Harry took up with a young beauty, and actually installed her in a home on the estate, though not, it seems probable, within the walls of Uppark, which would have shamed his mother. Her name was Emy Lyon, and she was to become in turn Amy Lyon, Emly or Emily Hart, Emma Hart and finally Emma, Lady Hamilton. The changes were as many and various as the draped 'Attitudes' which in later years she and Romney, the artist who painted her most frequently, made famous. Of all the people closely associated with Uppark she is perhaps the best known, for although some of her earlier history is obscure her attraction for posterity continues. This is scarcely to be wondered at since in the course of time she won the heart, not only of Sir Harry

51

Featherstonhaugh, but of his friend Charles Greville, of the British Minister to Naples, Sir William Hamilton, and of that exemplar of the fighting seaman, Admiral Lord Nelson.

Emma Hart, as she was probably known at the time when Sir Harry made her acquaintance, was born in April 1765 and was sixteen when she came under his protection. She had been born at Neston in Cheshire, and she was developing attributes which were not only to attract men, but to hold them. Her complexion was fair, her features classical, her figure buxom, and her power to please most evident. She was gay, vital, uninhibited—and she had nothing to lose but her looks.

Emma's father, a blacksmith, died when she was a baby, but the care given to her by her mother and grandmother, both remarkable women, lacked nothing in practical attention. Her mother, who later passed under the name of Mrs Cadogan, saw to it that she learnt to read and write, although to the end of her life her spelling remained wildly individual. When Sir Harry met her first, she had migrated to London, where she had been in domestic service. Later she found more exciting employment with a certain Dr James Graham, whose 'Temple of Health' situated in the Adelphi facing the Temple, offered means of "prolonging Human Life, Healthily and Happily to the very longest possible Period of Human Existence." Emma played a part in one or other of the various tableaux which were a feature of Graham's establishment.

Although there is no shadow of doubt that Emma was a girl whose morals were assailable, and one whose mother, then as later, took a strictly realistic view of the value of her beauty, there can be little support for the idea that Emma had already had a child when Sir Harry began to pay his attentions. The theory rests upon the fact that in the Harting registers there is an entry for April 7, 1781: "Buried Francis Lyon." This entry has led to the notion that Emma's first illegitimate child died on the Uppark estate, and was interred locally. Emma's fullest biographer, the late Walter Sichel, never credited this, and her latest annalist, Mr Hugh Tours, went to the trouble of having the registers searched anew. This resulted in the discovery that the name Lyon occurs nearly two years earlier, when the burial of one Sarah Lyon took place, proof that the name was that of a family then living in the village.

While at Uppark or in its neighbourhood, Emma made herself thoroughly agreeable to Sir Harry and his friends, and as her stay lasted nearly a year, there were no doubt occasions when, in the absence of Lady Fetherstonhaugh, she may have graced the house itself. She may even have danced on the dining room table, as tradition maintains, though whether or not in a state of nature will never be known. Certainly her gaiety and her fearlessness, particularly on horseback, were admired by Sir Harry and his cronies, among whom was a rising young politician, the Honourable Charles Greville, who was to play a leading part in Emma's life.

Emma's departure from Uppark was as abrupt as her advent. In November 1781, when Sir Harry was at Leicester for the hunting, she was packed off to Cheshire, six months' pregnant, and with barely enough money for travelling expenses. She had undoubtedly been indiscreet, and although she appealed to him in vain for help, she never blamed Sir Harry for his conduct. Indeed, much later in life she turned to him once again, and this time not in vain.

The most important letter she ever wrote was addressed from Cheshire. It was to Greville, and it was the first of a number of uninhibited missives which Greville preserved throughout his life. They were first printed by Alfred Morrison in 1893 in a series of papers which he collected, mainly concerning the Hamilton and Nelson families.

Greville had evidently sent word to Emma to say that he might be able to help her, and he received the following reply on January 10, 1782. It was the first of a stream which continued over many years.

'Yesterday did I receve your kind letter. It put me in some spirits, for believe me, I am allmost distracktid. I have never heard from Sir H. and he is not at Lechster now. I am sure. What shall I dow? Good God. What shall I dow? I have wrote 7 letters, and no anser. I can't come to town for want of money. I have not a farthing to bless my self with, and I think my friends looks cooly on me. I think so. O.G. what shall I dow? what shall I dow? O how your letter affected me. wen you wished me happiness. O.G. that I was in your possession or was in Sir H. What a happy girl would I have been! "Girl indeed." what else am I but a girl in distress—in reall distress. For God's sake, G, write

the minet you get this, and only tell me what I am to dow.
Direct same whay. I am allmos mad. O, for God's sake, tell me
what is to become of me. O dear Grevell, write to me. Write to
me. G, adue, and believe yours for ever.

'Don't tell my mother what distress I am in, and dow afford
me some comfort . . . '

It would have been a cold creature indeed who could have
resisted such a call. Greville responded, to their mutual benefit.
After advising Emma to make it up with Sir Harry, or else
to sever this and every other connection for good, he promised
to look after her and her coming child. He had a house at
Paddington and there, Emma and her mother were shortly afterwards installed.

Emma suited Greville perfectly, and for some years, made him
very happy, but his intention was to bring off a rich marriage.
In 1786, after much argument and difficulty, he managed to ship
Emma off to his rich widower uncle, Sir William Hamilton, then
and for many years to come resident at Naples. Emma would
probably have been faithful to Greville to his dying day if he
had allowed her to be so, but Greville, though capable of an
occasional impulsive kindness, was not a man to saddle himself
permanently with a mistress who could bring him only physical
comfort.

In so far as Sir Harry Fetherstonhaugh was concerned, there
was a long span of time before Emma renewed her acquaintance.
When she did so, it was after fate had dealt hardly with both of
them.

For a few years after Emma's departure, Sir Harry seems to
have been content with hunting and roystering, but he had
enough of his father's sense of public duty to wish to follow him
into Parliament, although it was not until the year 1782 that
he found a seat. Sir Matthew's old constituents at Portsmouth
showed no favour to his widow's half-brother, Joseph Iremonger,
who would have been glad to succeed him, or to Sir Harry
himself, who was unsuccessful at elections held in 1777 and
three years later.

In 1782, with the backing of Lord Rockingham and others,
he was at last returned. He entered Parliament as a member of
the party of Charles James Fox, who was in opposition. This

affiliation was natural enough in a man who was already a member of the circle which surrounded the Prince of Wales, who was later to become successively, Prince Regent, and King George IV. William Pitt was Prime Minister, and very much the King's first servant. George, Prince of Wales followed the tradition of his family and gave his support to the political party which was out of office. He found only nominal support from Sir Harry, who discovered that attendance at Westminster was abominably irksome, remained as silent on public issues as his father had always been, and in 1796, when another election was impending, declined to stand again. A letter which he wrote to his supporters put his reasons for withdrawing cogently enough.

'The fact is,' he said, in a disillusioned way, 'that from the corruption of the times the House of Commons in its present degraded state is such a complete farce, that I am quite disgusted with being one of the puppets; were there any prospect of redress I would not retire; but I am indignant to the last degree at the insult offered to all people of common sense and a love for the constitution by those who have left us only the shadow without the substance.'

It was sport that the heir to the throne looked for from Sir Harry, and he did not look in vain. In 1784 and 1785, he stayed at Uppark for three days' racing on West Harting Down, bringing with him his jockey, Sir John Lade, famous for his bad language, and Lady Lade, a woman whose tongue matched her husband's. The appropriate entry in the *Racing Calendar* runs as follows:

'1784

'On Tuesday the 17th August H.R.H. the Prince of Wales's *Merry Traveller* 8st 7 lb beat Sir H. Fetherston's *Rockingham*, 8st the last quarter of a mile for 100 gs.

'Sir H. Fetherston's *Don Josef*, rode by himself, beat H.R.H. the Prince of Wales's *Hermit*, rode by Sir John Lade, over the course for 50 gs.

'H.R.H. the Prince of Wales's *Merry Traveller*, rode by Mr. Delme, beat Sir John Lade's *Medleycot*, rode by Major Hanger, over the Course for 50 gs.

'Sir H. Fetherston's *Speranza*, rode by Col. Tarleton, beat

Col. Sheldon's *Bustard*, rode by Major Hanger, over the Course for 50 gs.'

Sir Harry entertained the Prince on a lavish scale. Records of the ample preparations for the royal party made by Lady Fetherstonhaugh and listed in every detail in her own handwriting, show that she took stock of every item. The Prince brought his own horses to race on 'The most beautiful Spot of Ground I believe that England can produce . . . ', as Miss Iremonger wrote after she and her aunt, Lady Fetherstonhaugh 'had come to Wherwell from Uppark to vacate our places to the Prince and his Party . . . ' She added, ' . . . Three Hot made Dishes of meat were to form a regular part of each morning's breakfast if the Duc de Chartres came. I suppose we shall have him at Bath at the end of the year to correct Indigestion.'

'Prinny' may have discoursed on the triumphs that his chef could produce under the palm-headed columns of the Brighthelmstone Pavilion kitchen but when Moget of the Uppark kitchens was put upon his mettle he must have proved himself a master chef to compete with the following list in the space of three days. Lady Fetherstonhaugh entered:

'Upward of 80 in family besides the people that come in every day—3 days entertainment in Aug. 1784 for the Prince of Wales 12 in Company . . . '

Her estimates were generous:

'2 Bucks, a Welsh sheep, a doz. Ducks,—4 Hams, dozens of Pigeons, and Rabbits, Flitches of Bacon, Lobsters and Prawns; a Turtle of 120 lbs.; 166 lbs. of Butter; 376 Eggs, 67 Chickens; 23 Pints of Cream, 30 lbs. of Coffee, 10 lbs. of Fine Tea; and three lbs. of common tea.'

These are among the items which cover 109 lines of closely written stores. The list of wines included Hock, Madeira, Lisbon, '41 Port; 7 Brandy; 1½ Hold of strong Beer; while Musick cost £26 5s 0d and another chef to assist Moget cost £25; another 2 Bucks added cost £11; 2 more sheep cost only £2 10s, and another 2 carp £1 10s 0d.' In addition to all this, the 'Country Butcher's bill for Hams and Tongues'; amount to £10 4s 9d, and 34 lbs. of Lemons must have brought a pleasant dash of colour to this mountain of provender. Fifty pounds of sugar were ordered; a sack of wheat and fine flour cost £1 15s 0d, fifty-eight chickens were 10d each; truffles cost £3 3s 9d.

A dozen wax candles were 'taken out of the Store room' for one day. They dined in the White and Gold Dining Room, and there was a fine display of plate: gilt dessert dishes by William Homer, Tazzas by Benjamin Pyne and Anthony Nelme, salvers of Peaston, the latest set of gilt candelabra by Ben Laver and Davenport, with the addition of the tall gilt Prince's Racing Cup, won by Sir Harry, which is at Uppark to this day.

In August 1784, Mrs Montagu, well known as a Blue Stocking, remarked of the party:

'The P. of W. has been at Sir Harry Fetherstones, he staid three days, during which they had races of all sorts—fine horses — poneys — cart-horses — women — and men in sacks, with various other divertimenti fit for children of six foot high. I hear he was much delighted and said that Newmarket Races were dull in comparison. They were within three or four miles of us, but no one except servants went from hence, nor do I find that any ladies of fashion in the town were at them. Poor Lady Featherstone, Sir Henry's mother, fled from the riot to M. Iremonger's. These pretty sports attracted a great mob, who were charm'd with a P. so familiarly affable to them all.'

In July 1785, racing was at one moment jeopardised by the Regent's impulsive request for Sir Harry to proceed to Westminster to vote. He wrote hurriedly from Brighton, urging his friend to vote against a measure of Pitt's.

'My dear Sir Harry,
I have just received the enclosed Letter by Express from London; will you allow me to offer my advice on this occasion; If you have not already got a pair off in this business I wd go to London as to Night and endeavour to get one early To Morrow morning, by wh. means you will be back again with us in the Evening and ready for the Terrible Terrible work with the High Bred cattle, that is to ensue the next morning, pray take Onslow with you upon the same errand. If you should have the least idea of postponing the party till after Brighton Races I shd (wish) to hear from you, and that you wd. send all our Horses back,

however if I hear nothing from you I shall certainly come to Dinner to Up Park Tomorrow. I assure you my dear Featherstone I am exceedingly concerned at this *contretemps* however I think with a little trouble you will be able *de le surmonter.*

Believe my dear friend, ever most truly yours

George P.

Brighton. Wednesday. ½ past one o clock.

July 20th.

1785.

P.S. Forgive this scrawl as I not only write in ye strongest terms but with a Pen wh can hardly write.'

Racing was not Sir Harry's only diversion—there was also whist. Items in the account books are losses of £812 at this game, and on stakes at Lewes Races, but over the same period he won £1,374: So he was well in hand. At whist he defeated the Duke of York to the tune of £85, an account which is put down 'unpaid'. He won £549 on one stake at the Lewes Races in August. Later in the year he lost £2,580, which included £250 over a match with Chanticlair. In the same year and for the same period he won £2,992.

How hectic was the social whirl in which he was swept up is well illustrated by the following, taken from his account book:

'Come to Town March 29th. Saddle horses next day: Went to Uppark 13th April, returning the 17th. To Uppark the 29th. Four saddle horses got to Newmarket the 22nd.—Two came away the 27th. Returned to Town the 6th May—to Newmarket the 8th; to Woburn the 15th; to London the 18th; to Newmarket the 22nd; to London the 29th; to the Oaks the 8th May; to London the 10th.'

It was always an easy matter for the Prince to drive over the Downs from Brighton in his yellow carriage, to stay at Uppark with Sir Harry, and he enjoyed so doing. The Prince's room is pannelled, and facing west. He preferred this to any other and wrote asking to have it:

'Dear Sir Harry,

I hope you will not think me very troublesome if I beg of you to give me my old Bed at Up Park on Sunday night. I shall endeavour to be with you by dinner between five and six o'clock. Nobody but General Hulse will come with me. I am

very sincerely Yours

George P.

Brighton;
August 14th 1795.'

No doubt the Prince was accompanied on this intimate visit not only by General Hulse, but with the inseparable little dogs whose presence at Uppark has been identified by the traditional hall marks left on the foot of the curtains of the Prince's damask bed. It took fourteen months to repair this bed, which was restored completely, within the room itself. The furniture in the Regent's day included the Chinese lacquer cabinets now on the staircase. The Regent's dogs were tied to the leg of one of them and, it is said, broke it.

While Sir Harry was ruffling it in London, racing at Newmarket, or hunting with the Quorn, life at Uppark continued on a more tranquil course. There are descriptions of how Lady Fetherstonhaugh and her niece, Miss Iremonger, spent their time. Miss Iremonger, who was a frequent visitor, wrote letters, mainly of gossip, to her friend, Miss Heber, of Weston, in Northamptonshire. In 1786 she reported:

' . . . Mr Savile is engaged to Miss Willoughby, Daughter of Lord Middleton. At present He meets with obstructions but lives upon Hopes, & I wish they may answer. His Taste for Musick continues & he has brought here with him Signor Soderini, one of the Principal Violin Players from the Opera, to instruct him, so that every evening my Pianoforte takes its share with the two Violins, & we form a Concert which I think a delightful rational amusement.'

The Pianoforte and the old Opera scores are still at Uppark to recall those times.

Sir Harry, for all his wild ways, showed his mother the utmost consideration and gratitude for all she did for him. In August 1786, Miss Iremonger wrote from Uppark:

' . . . this Country has always peculiar Charms; there is nothing like it & I am always sorry to quit it. We enjoyed the few hot Days and evenings during the last moon very much;

My Aunt & I frequently drove in the Harvest-fields by moon-light, in an open Carriage, & supped at our return by the same light, without Candles. Perhaps you did not suspect I was such a Lunatick.'

Lady Fetherstonhaugh died at Wherwell at the age of sixty-six. In her mother's first married home she had always found the affectionate attachment of her half-brothers a constant source of contentment, and to them she turned in her last illness; she died in December 1788. Miss Iremonger was with her in a place they both loved, built on the banks of the Test, astride the river, where the trout are still fed from a kitchen window.

Miss Heber was told by Miss Iremonger:

' . . . She had been a tender Parent to me the greater part of my life, & the more I reflect upon what she was to me, the more I must feel for myself. That I was able to be of use to her in her last illness & to watch her expiring Hour is my greatest comfort.

'So did Sir Harry with the utmost tenderness, which I was sure gave her the highest satisfaction as long as She was sensible, & it is but justice to him to say that He has shown the most poignant Grief on this occasion, & I believe, is truly conscious of a loss that can never be repaired to him . . . '

It was not in the young baronet's nature to live a retired life and he was soon back in royal society. But the saying: 'Put not your trust in princes,' was never more appropriate than in the present case. Prinny tired of Sir Harry, or may even have quarrelled with him: the affair is wrapped in mystery. What is certain is that shortly after his mother's death Sir Harry began to be seen less in the Prince's circle, and not much in general society. The fact made him bitter. He later confessed that he had begun an account of his life in *le grand monde*. If he per-severed, discretion caused him to destroy his efforts. What survives is a series of references, sometimes acid, to pleasures past, and suggestions of regret for a life which he had once enjoyed.

That the Prince was also conscious of estrangement, and regretted it, is proved by a letter which survives from a few years later. This reads:

'Dear Featherstone,
I hope that you never will conceive that I can ever think

that you can entertain two opinions about me, or that I can entertain two opinions about you. The sincere Wish of my heart is that upon the finding of friendship, upon which we have ever liv'd, and I trust ever shall live through life, you are at perfect liberty whatever is most convenient or suitable to Yourself but I should feel most unhappy if my Home is at any moment of my Life open to the reception of my friends, that an invitation should not be sent to you, who I consider as one of the first and firmest

Ever affectionately Yours
George P.

Brighton.
Jany. 29th 1804.
P.S. Send me the Old Major without fail and spare Welch if you can.'

Just over two years after this letter, Sir Harry was reminded of Emma, now Emma Hamilton, by one of those distracted and undated letters with which that character was accustomed to astonish her friends.

Since she had left Uppark to return to Cheshire, Emma had known bewildering changes. Sir William Hamilton, after living with her for five years, at first as his somewhat reluctant mistress (since she was truly devoted to Greville), had then married her, and she had reigned many years at the British Embassy in Naples and in her husband's other houses. Then, after the battle of the Nile, Nelson, whom she had already met, brought his victorious squadron to Naples, and she had ministered to him so attentively that he had become her slave for life. Old Sir William had died after the three of them had returned home together in 1800. A joint household had been set up at Merton, near Wimbledon, and soon afterwards Nelson himself had taken over command of the Mediterranean Fleet, an appointment, which was eventually to lead to the campaign of Trafalgar and to his death in action in the hour of victory.

The whole Emma Hamilton-Nelson story was familiar, most of it through newspaper reports, and the rest from gossip. Emma's child, Emma Carew, brought up under Greville's protection, and the result of his liaison while at Uppark, was then a young woman of twenty-five and she had gone abroad, possibly as a governess, to be heard of no more. Horatia, Emma's child by Nelson, was then five years old, and living with her mother at Merton as 'Lord Nelson's adopted daughter.' The hero had left money for Horatia's care and maintenance, and he had also left Emma comfortably provided for, giving her the Merton property. But Emma, left to herself, was always improvident, as her letter to Sir Harry showed clearly enough. This ran:

'My dear Sir Harry,

If you cannot do what I ask you burn this and say you cannot for I shall attribute your inability to the Right Course and be assured I shall not take it ill.

I have Two Thousand pounds coming to me from Earl Nelson but as things are in Chancery it may be Xmas before I Receive if you could lend me five hundred pounds be assured it will at this moment be of the greatest use as I am arranging my affairs and *you shall* surely have it the moment I am paid or when I sell Merton if ever you did be content with a Bill on Coutts for Xmas I shall then have money in my Hands but I cannot bear the Idea to have the appearance of begging for a moment as I never did not perhaps never shall have an occasion to do it again Lord St Vincent is to speak to Mr Fox and will give testimony of my services and has profest great friendship for *me so that I hope* but only be assured I ask you at a moment sooner than pay an Extravagant interest on Borrowing and pray let us meet as tho I had not ask'd this favour from you and let me come to Up Park for a few days to speak of old times perhaps long before that time I shall have repaid you—indeed I feel at this moment more than I can tell you in asking this favour but let it be as it may I shall ever feel your obliged.

ever most grateful,
E.H.

Burn this.

If you do me this favour let me know by a Line E goes to night but she is taken care of in case of any accident pray write that I may not think you angry.'

Emma's reference to 'Earl Nelson' was to the seaman's brother and heir, a cleric capable of generosity only to himself, and Emma was hoping, by the influence of such people as Lord St Vincent, Fox and others, to secure the revision of Sir William

Hamilton's pension, or else to receive something from the Government for her services at Naples. She was to be disappointed. Nelson's legacies, considerable as they were, did not prove to be enough; the government did nothing for her, and some nine years later she was to die in exile in Calais, in debt and with her affairs hopelessly involved.

Meanwhile, Sir Harry acted promptly and with generous consideration, though his letter to his old flame has not survived. His kindness naturally made Emma delighted, and she wrote at once to acknowledge the good deed.

'Merton Thursday 6 o Clock
Your letter my Dear Sir Harry has made me *very happy* I write from bed very unwell having had a little fever all night I was agitated yesterday with Lord St Vincent's kindness and allso last evening with parting for a time from a very *amiable naive good good* Hearted person whose Health requires air and Exercise her tears & really sorrow at parting *un mand'd* me for I do not know that I feel more at parting with any friend than I did with her . . . I shall be in town tomorrow by one will you call on me that I may give you my thanks and if you let me have it in a letter instead of going to Coutts I shall be obliged to you as it is to pay household that I am giving up & I will give you a note on Coutts I shall be rich enough one of these days when they do something for me and their debts paid to me but you have at this moment made my mind easy.

to me that never owed nor probably shall again it made me completely uneasy and I wish to do all that cou'd be comfortable to *our* friend *who be assured* in case of accident is provided for and she is gone into the country happy

ever believe me my Dear Sir Harry your affectionate gratefull
E.H.

Excuse this written from bed.'

Emma enclosed with this letter an IOU dated as follows:

'London July 3rd 1806
Messrs. Coutts and Co
    please pay Sir Harry Featherston five hundred pounds nine months after date. from your Humble servant
Emma Hamilton.'

Sir Harry never presented Emma's note to Messrs. Coutts, and it remains preserved with her letters to him, a pleasing memorial to his warmth of heart. Emma's 'amiable, naive, good good Hearted person' was possibly her daughter, Emma Carew, and the death a few years later of Mrs. Cadogan, Emma's mother, was the occasion of another note from Sir Harry, full of sympathy.

In the year 1810, George III became permanently insane, and his elder son became Prince Regent, with the cares of State to absorb what attention he could bring himself to spare from matters more trivial. Sir Harry still had friends at Court, among them Henry William Paget, later Marquess of Anglesey, who, so Sir Harry told a crony, took up his cause at a dinner at Kew 'in the most full and decided manner'. He added that this was 'a great satisfaction to myself, however prejudiced and poisoned the royal party etc., appeared to be against me'.

'When I contemplate my own situation,' he wrote in 1811, 'I am more surprised at being able to bear it as I do; for all the finest aphorisms in the world afford but slender comfort under a *malheur sans remede*'. In his misery he even began to make a collection of the more vicious lampoons and caricatures of his former friend, of which, both then and later, there was no lack. Prinny's corpulence made him an easy target, and so did his extravagance at a time when there was much suffering in the country, and when a full-scale war against Napoleon demanded sacrifices from all sections of society.

The Regent's own military activities moved Sir Harry to comment to Paget in October 1811 that the august person was expected shortly at Brighton 'and report says for the purpose of a military tour and a visit to Portsmouth'. In another letter he assured a friend that Paget would 'show his influence, for my enemies, God help them, have been great and numerous'. He added that 'nothing . . . will ever again draw me from retirement'.

Sir Harry might be 'retired', but he was still acutely sensitive to even the most extravagant gossip, circulated, as he supposed, by his 'enemies'. In January 1812 he wrote to Paget:

'The Regent told Mrs Fitzherbert some little time since that his two pages, du Pasquier and Jouard, had SEEN me riding about the streets of London in disguise—broad flapped hat, horseman's coat, and immense whiskers. He asserted it so roundly that she asked Day at Brighton if it was true. It is laughable yet provoking . . . he will make it go down under all circumstances to MY DISADVANTAGE.'

A few months earlier, he had been chagrined at his exclusion from a splendid fete given by the Regent at Carlton House. 'All London will be there,' he noted sadly, 'and be dressed magnificently; and of course WE shall not be of it.'

He consoled himself by reporting the adverse or critical comments which friends sent him after the occasion.

'A propos of this wonderful fete, you will have seen in the papers, and heard from others all about it. I have seen Charles [Paget] who is in raptures, and in my opinion would willingly have prolonged his stay in Town for some minor ones, had not Mrs Paget been obliged to return a week before him to Fair Oak, of which I never knew a word. In a letter I had from the Duke of Bedford . . . he observes "the fete was very magnificent, very hot and very disagreeable". Most people would probably think it all charming. Thomas [Tyrwhitt] says he never stirred from the outer hall (his station), and when supper was announced, went home to bed, that the whole was splendid beyond conception, and the Regent's new Field Marshal's uniform *wonderful!* He also says "my friend Cholmondley must have been disappointed, as it seems there was no room at the Prince's table lower than a Marquis, and he is comparatively a young Earl, so he will be more displeased than ever at Addington's not having made him a Marquis; his two particular friends and frequenters of his house, Keppel and Hammond, are laughing at him to everyone, for it seems he was much vexed at not having had the management of this fete, and as it proves, it could not have succeeded better".

'Mrs Fitzherbert was *not* present. It was signified to her that her rank would not admit of her being at the Regent's table, and she took her line accordingly. He seems to have designed a marked hint to poor Napoleon of his intention again to place a Bourbon on the throne of France by so distinguished and public a reception of the family. He may in my opinion just now do *anything but that,* for his god-like virtues are in every one's

mouth, and breathe a proud defiance to all who are not disposed
to join in such senseless adulation. I always felt sure it would be
so, even when he has been whining to *us* about his *un*-merited
want of popularity. Nothing can have exceeded the *éclat*
through-out of Paget's reception, which you will rejoice in as
much as myself, and of which you will of course have heard
more. In this at least I feel the Regent has exercised a sound
judgment.'

Berkeley Paget, describing the Regent's uniform, wrote that:

'Not only the Cuffs, Collars and Front of the Coat were richly
embroidered but the very seams — all the seams ! ! ! On a
moderate calculation it must have cost and weighed in pounds
sterling and avoirdupois at least 200.

'*Mon petit Graves* is solely occupied during the morning in
instructing Ladies in cotillons and in the evening in dancing
them . . . Tho' in size somewhat similar one cannot well com-
pare him to Shakespear's Elephant in *Troilus and Cressida*.'

It is a tribute both to Sir Harry and his friends that their
devotion survived the strains of this difficult period in his life.
The Pagets clearly regarded his position with great sympathy.
In 1811, Captain Charles Paget wrote to his brother Arthur:

'I am going to see Fetherstone. Poor fellow. I see no better hope
for him and I can't feel patience with the Duke of Bedford for
his cool and indifferent conduct . . . He never even mentioned
Fetherstone's name, much less desired me to deliver any kind of
message to him . . . '

The Bedfords, it is good to know, eventually returned to Sir
Harry and visited him later in the year. It must have been at
this time that the Bedford Sundial was placed in the walled
Kitchen Garden and the Bedford Vase was proudly placed in
the Saloon. In his turn, Sir Harry sent them gifts of buck and
pheasant.

Left to his own devices, Sir Harry turned to the consolations
of the countryman. Here, he had to admit:

'Notwithstanding my own indolence (which is more or less
owing to a sick and wounded *mind*) there is no pursuit affording
more rational amusement or more solid advantages in country
retirement than the management of a farm . . . '

He tried hard, with this persuasive comment, to induce Arthur Paget to buy himself an estate near Uppark, but without success.

He continued to take great pride and interest in horseflesh and wrote to a friend in May 1811:

'In consequence of your determination I shall send "Mathilde" off tomorrow and write Paget a line to desire that he will give directions about her to Tattersall. She is quite sound and her legs fine, but her old coat is not sufficiently off to show her exactly as I could have wished. You have certainly done right, for independent of other circumstances she is not in my opinion likely to be a pleasant one to ride. I did not however mean to pronounce it to you till the fact was more clearly ascertained; something is to be ascribed to great awkwardness, but there is an inherent lack of *good* action. This accounts for *my* declining your kind offer.'

Sport was his solace. 'Famous sport at Uppark,' wrote the Duke of Argyll, '408 pheasants in 4 days, and 835 things.' What the 'things' were is, alas, uncertain.

In another letter Sir Harry wrote:
'Delmé and I take our guns every morning, and always have some fun. What do you think of his killing a gold pheasant yesterday by mistake? Joseph Manton has also been here; he killed a pied pheasant and was very near killing me . . . '

He continued:

'As the Duke of Bedford has announced his intention of coming here towards the end of the month, I mean to regulate the battues accordingly . . . ' (January 9, 1812)

Sir Harry had decided views on how such parties should be conducted, as he confided to the ever-patient Arthur Paget on October 21, 1811:

'After all that rain, what delightful weather since! which I have been enjoying in my usual mode, that of lounging, for I have hardly used my gun except to kill a few young pheasants for Lady Sefton. It is not *quite* so bad a year for them below the hill as Barton announced, and Eames thinks it better than the last with him, but as the hedge-row shooting in autumn depends upon a *productive* season (at least to have it in perfection), I

don't like a less lively thing than usual. Charles is certainly out
of luck this should happen a.d. 1811, and I infinitely more regret
it on his account than my own, for I really can amuse myself
very well without that incessant discharge of field-pieces so
essential to all fashionable sportsmen of the present generation.'

This letter gives one of the writer's many reactions to the
state of the weather. Like many Englishmen, especially country-
men, he was extremely sensitive to changes of climate, which
affected him both mentally and physically.

In May 1811, he wrote:

'The last two days have been delicious! Nothing but slush-pot
with a vengeance till then for this last fortnight, tho' thanks to
the chalky soil, my temporary bridge has not been carried away.'

In June, he wrote:

'It will be said that the weather continued favourable *only* for
the completion of the fête; in truth ever since it has been most
winter-like, and has *unhinged* me as usual.'

Two months later, in August, he exults:

'This is *quite* my weather and both body and mind partake of its
benefits. *Je suis à mon aise et toujours, . . .* '

While in January he complains:

'*Quel temps* ! I never remember so severe a beginning, whatever
the end may be. Yet it is felt more in London, and then, there is
the comfort in campagne of not having to go out *aprés le répas.*'

He wrote long gossipy letters to his friends, commenting on
political news, society hearsay and the latest translations of the
classics. He did his best to persuade himself that he was better
off as he was, aloof from the great world:

'The Newmarket meetings have been hitherto flat; large parties
and deep Whist at Cheveley; Brummell and Alvanley the losers.
I never hear or read of these grand parties, which are represented
as almost a *chef d'ouvre* for Aladdin's lamp, that I don't hug
myself on not being one of them. I am amusing myself with
beginning 'my *reminiscences pendant un séjour de 35 ans dans*

ce qu'on apelle le grand monde : But they shall not be published till after my exit.'

To distract himself, and perhaps in unconscious emulation of the Prince Regent, he began to plan improvements to his home. In this way, Humphry Repton was introduced to Uppark and the last notable changes were made to the house.

IV

Correspondence
with Humphry Repton

Sir Harry Fetherstonhaugh had never been devoid of taste, and his love for things French, deriving from his early Tour, increased rather than diminished as a result of the difficulties and sometimes the impossibility of Continental travel resulting from the war with Revolutionary and Napoleonic France which had begun in 1793 and which continued, with only one short break, until 1814.

The break occurred at the Peace of Amiens. This afforded a breathing space—it proved to be no more—during the years 1802-3. Sir Harry, in common with many others, took advantage of the lull to make a journey to Paris. He chose the right time, since had he travelled a little later he would have been interned: for the war re-opened suddenly, and many hundreds were caught, and kept, on the wrong side of the Channel in the earlier months of 1803. Incidentally, there was little reciprocal curiosity on the French side, for it is a delusion that the English are, and always have been, the most insular people in Europe.

French society in 1802 was not what it was—too many had perished at the guillotine, or in battle; but there were art treasures to be had at reasonable prices, and Sir Harry was able to acquire a writing desk, once the property of Queen Marie Antoinette, and a Sèvres vase of great beauty, garlanded with flowers in the pre-Revolutionary style. This had been added to: a cover of gilt ormolu, on which was enthroned a cupid holding a captive dove in a cage surmounting it. The vase was supported by ormolu tortoises, the juxtaposition of two inharmonious styles in a single piece being startling evidence of current debasement in taste.

Sir Harry also added Sèvres vases by Mirault, whose name he inscribed in ink on the base. He kept the receipts, which are still at Uppark. He also brought back from France exquisite furniture, destined to sink with the *Titanic* on its way to the New York Metropolitan Museum in 1912.

Despite the recent and protracted hostilities, Frenchmen welcomed the English Milords as they flocked to the capital city to savour pleasures long-denied. Some, like Talleyrand, who invited Sir Harry to dine with him, were doubtless delighted to renew old contacts or to make acquaintance with men who had been denied the experience of egalitarianism, followed by a military dictatorship. Sir Harry kept his invitations, which included one from the Minister for War. This was on paper headed *République française*. It carried the legend *Liberté* and *Egalité* and it was dated *Paris, le 15 Floréal an 11 de la République française, une et indivisible.*

The interlude in Paris, which was repeated later in Sir Harry's life, refreshed his enthusiasm for matters beyond sport and farming, and may well have turned his thoughts towards making changes in the house where he had lived all his life. He had the good sense to seek the advice of Humphry Repton, a man two years older than himself who had lost his fortune and turned landscape gardener. Repton was employed at some of the greater houses, and was always welcome by reason of his intelligence and wit. Repton's publications, his *Observations on the Theory and Practice of Landscape Gardening* (1803) and *An Enquiry into the Changes of Taste in Landscape Gardening* (1806) produced changes of fashion sensational in their own day, and of lasting interest.

Janeites will readily recall that Repton is introduced by name in the sixth chapter of *Mansfield Park*, where Miss Bertram remarks to Mr Rushworth, who is considering improvements at Sotherton Court: 'Your best friend upon such an occasion . . . would be Mr Repton, I imagine'. 'That is what I am thinking of,' was the reply. ' . . . I think I had better have him at once. His terms are five guineas a day.'

Sir Harry was in excellent company, and Repton was to provide him not only with a more accurate idea of terms than might be gathered from the pages of *Mansfield Park*, but with numerous ideas, embodied in a series of letters refreshingly wide in their range of topics, though sometimes highly odd in their expression. Repton was fifty-nine when he first came to Uppark in 1810, and was at the height of his fame and achievement. His sons shared their father's interests and at least some of his skill, and they helped him in his business. At Uppark, Repton's ideas concerned the house itself far more than the grounds, though the clumps of trees which were planted at his suggestion continue as a reminder of his principal interest.

Repton enjoyed writing letters, telling Sir Harry in 1815 that:

'In the busiest days of my life I have found relief from professional pursuits in the employment of my pen, and I shall leave a large mass to my executors to prove that leisure was irksome to me at all times . . . '

Another bond between the two men was that they were both aggrieved with the Regent. The matter was detailed, from Repton's point of view, in a letter he sent to Sir Harry in 1814. Repton had submitted designs, in 1808, for alterations at the Brighton Pavilion. What then transpired is related in the following rather breathless fashion:

'1808 — July 25th — attended at Carlton House by command from 12. till 5—in vain—July 26th ditto. During all this time I saw a great bustle of Carriages with Ladies and on the 27th was again desired to attend at 12.—when I was immediately admitted and can never forget the gracious manner in which the Prince said "Repton, I am sorry to have kept you two days in waiting but if I could tell you the business in which I have been engaged—you would hold me excused".

'The papers afterwards explained it under the title of "Delicate Investigation" — which like my own visit at Carlton House ended in nothing — for myself — H.R.H. after expressing the most perfect satisfaction with all I propose—put it into the hands of the Surveyor General — [James Wyatt] because he could do it at the public expense and I was of course superseded —and since his death [1813]—he has appointed Nash to be Surveyor general which I had the fullest reason to expect from his having mentioned him with contempt and his warm economiums of all I have proposed at Brighton—when my hopes of future eminence were blown like an empty bladder—or the bubble of a Child—

'And after seeing the only man on earth with whom I had ever quarrelled raised to the situation to which I reasonably aspired—I can only say—Cursed is the man who puts his trust in princes—and so ended my Royal hopes—at this time my son George who is connected with Nash and shares his profits if not his honours—is actually at Portsmouth preparing for a Royal and Imperial visit by new furnishing the Government house and I should have been there and when so near — probably at Uppark—! Alas no!'   (June 9th 1814)

In preparing plans for the improvements at Uppark, Repton was aware of the special charms of the house with which he had to deal; 'but what rarity can retain its rareness at Uppark where all that is good is common—& all that is common is more than commonly good', he once asked. On another occasion, October 8, 1815, he wrote:

'I have sometimes endeavr'd to analyze the sources of the pleasure experienced during my late visit and I find no end to the Combination of Causes — all co-operating with the same effect.—Comfort Elegance—Magnificence—and Good Taste are the viands—while Hospitality is the Seasoning and as everything depends on Cookery I must pronounce that *La Cuisine est Parfaite chez vous*, and this you may take Literally or figuratively—being equally *positive Truth*.

'From objects of Taste—the transition to Smelling is natural —and I may truly say that in no place have I ever seen such accurate attention to olfactory joy as at Uppark—every room has its depot of odours for permanent use—while every window has its Orange Trees and Tuberoses—and admits perfume from the surrounding beds of Mignionette and Heliotrope—till the whole is an atmosphere of sweets—and though I do not indulge in the artificial and manufactured produce of the distillery—yet the Native fragrance of flowers fresh dispensing their aromatic treasures—may next to fruit be deem'd the great luxury of a garden—how different from the farmyard—the delight of the modern *Butcher Gentry*.'

As always, when engaged in work of this kind, Repton prepared one of his Red Books of elaborately and delicately coloured drawings of his plans. His Book on Uppark is thought to be one of the best of its kind. It was found in a shattered condition but it has now been restored to its former freshness by the Archive Office of Chichester. The drawings illustrate Repton's manuscript notes, and his well-known method of showing a site before and after 'improvement' carries the reader back to the mid-eighteenth-century lay-out of Sir Matthew Fetherstonhaugh's Uppark, and forward into the Regency world of the by now middle-aged Sir Harry.

While acknowledging that little improvement was possible, Repton maintained that 'the [original] architect intended the north front not to be seen'. He and Sir Harry now decided to make this the principal entrance. Repton therefore designed a portico supported by pillars of Portland stone, connected to the main part of the house by a long corridor. In a letter of February 13, 1811, Repton explained the details of this improvement:

'The Portico is as much closed as it well can be with good effect —and you will observe that all external air will be effectually excluded by the several doors which occur in this passage of communication—and which will give great apparent depth and magnificence to the entrance—you will also observe that we have provided a way for the servants without lessening the Servants Hall, and with as little alteration as possible—it is only the labour of a little more excavation when we are lowering the ground to give a due elevation to this "façade"—on the roof of the Portico some expense may be saved if we use instead of lead Lord Stanhope's cement which costs little more than $\frac{1}{3}$.'

Repton thought that:

'A Mahogany Door in the Portico will be too mark'd a feature and cut the corridor in two—it would be better if oak or deal and painted a quiet—not a paper white.'

This door is at Uppark now, still in its packing case.

Repton intended to connect the Portico to the two flanking outbuildings erected by Sir Matthew, in about 1770, to replace the older blocks by screens of columns, a plan which proved too expensive.

On January 5, 1812, Repton sent:

'Designs for the Grates over the Areas—which if you approve

them—Mr Garthorne may send to Underwood and Doyle in Holborn will get them cast or perhaps there may be some iron foundry nearer and more commodious.'

These grates were to admit ventilation to the underground passages which linked the stables and kitchens with the house. It was intended to mount a lamp outside the house in the centre of the grates. The latter were put in but not the lamp. Of the lamp, Repton had written in the same letter:

'With respect to the central lamp post—I hoped you might have had a sufficient quantity of stone left and that the expense of labour would not have been quite so much—but matters of ornament and taste must be expensive—or they had better be wholly omitted and I should prefer a total omission of the lamp to one of much less importance—perhaps the best way would be to finish the centre with a stone five or six inches deep and pave the circle flat—on which a tripod of cast iron—bronzed might be at any time placed as a meuble.'

One of the notable features about Repton's work was that he succeeded in making a vantage point of the long side of Uppark. Visitors arriving through the Golden Gates at the head of the drive are confronted with a puzzling deflection of the carriage-way. The objective which Repton sought to emphasize as a salient point was the massive block of the western side of the north face where it projects in a wing from the main rectangle of the building.

To reach Uppark through the village of Harting, Repton insisted that a lodge should replace an old tanner's yard. The drive through the lovely beech woods passed bathing pools, where Repton built a gothic temple. This northern approach debouched on to the then newly-made road from Harting to Compton. Crossing this road, another lodge was built in which the night watchman of Uppark was installed. Thence the way climbed through a steep cutting into the north face of the down, bringing the visitor to the crest of the hill; passing through a narrow passage of beeches, the Golden Gates were reached which led by a gentle decline to the house.

Amongst other improvements planned by Repton outside the house was a Linnaeus Garden. Repton explained:

'There is a sketch for finishing the tiparian garden very different from what I fancied might be possible—as I had somewhere read of a whimsical arrangement of plants made by Linnaeus in such order that a Dial or clock was produced by the time of opening and shutting of certain flowers. I have corresponded with my friend Dr Smith, F.L.S., on this subject, who thinks Linnaeus failed in his attempt to procure a succession for any length of time—therefore we must give it up.'

(January 5, 1812)

Outstanding features of his work were the Game Larder and the Dairy. In one of his letters he drew a charming picture of how artistically game birds of every description and size could hang on pendant rods and brackets in a circular game house lined with white tiles, explaining:

'The game may be so disposed that the windows may all be left to a certain degree unencumbered, something in this way—and then one two four six or all eight compartments may be filled according as there are more or less to be displayed.'

(July 6, 1812)

The backbone knuckles of deer border the pebbled path which leads to this fascinating game house.

Repton was loath to give up all idea of making the pleasure grounds eventually laid out to increase the 'olfactory joys' of Uppark:

'And this little garden may either be laid out as I have hinted—or in plain square beds as a flower nursery, in which case it would be more of a Working garden but I think it ought to form a part of the dressed Pleasure Ground and the beds might be edged with a very deep box clipped to two feet high. The contrast betwixt this parterre and that in which the fruits and rock plants are proposed to prevail will increase the interest of both,—and I hope convince you that Uppark and its Comforts have not been out of my memory—and we have laid by all other matters that these might be submitted to Their Graces good taste and indeed I know nobody who possesses more of it . . . '

The ducal reference was almost certainly to the Bedfords and Argylls, who had recently stayed at Uppark and were interested in all that was proposed.

Repton's charges were specified in a letter written in March 1814, in which he states that his terms were '50 guineas each visit—and 5% on the architectural expenditure—giving credit for payments on account'. The formal correspondence in which this explanation appears, and the statement of account which was attached to it, give a concise summary of the actual times of Repton's visits, and of the sums which Sir Harry laid out in altering his property.

'Harestreet near Romford.

Sir,   March 2nd 1814

At my return last night from Dorsetshire Longleate etc. I found the honor of your letter dated February 13—and will no longer delay sending the papers which I received from Mr Higgins—and which will be sent in a parcel by the coach— . . . as it seems to be your wish to bring the accounts to a close . . . if I could regret anything it would be that there should be an account betwixt us of a nature where the obligation is so much on my side.—This letter is so decidely a Letter of business that I will not draw it out like the letters I enclose from Mr Higgins, the Measurer who writes without Measure—

I have the honour to be sir—
Your most obedient
humble servant
(signed) H. REPTON.'

The Account was as follows:

'Statement of Account betwixt Sir H. Featherstone, Bart., and H. and G. Repton.

1810—August Visit— Report on plans				
for ground.	£52.10.—	Aug. 22nd—Pd on Acc.		10. 0. 0.
	£42. 0. 0.	1811—Oct 3rd—ditto		£10. 0. 0.
1811—September visit—	£52.10. 0.	A draft on acc.		£100. 0. 0.
1812—May 19th pd Wallinger for				
Portland Stone	£138. 1. 6.	1812—April 6th. Chk on Drummonds		£250. 0. 0.
1812—Oct. visit	£52.10. 0.	Oct. 10th. Pd on acc.		£20. 0. 0.
1813—August visit	£52.10 0	1813—August 21st.		
		Dft.—		£100. .0. 0.
Paid Underwood and Doyle—	£91.15. 0.	Pd on acc.—		£20. 0. 0.
Commission on £4,200 expended		Balance		
according to	£210. 0. 0.			£181.16. 6.
Higgins, letter 31st January, 1814				
	£691.16. 6.			£691.16. 6.
	181.16. 6			

What might be called the incidentals of the Repton correspondence were scarcely less interesting than those relating the
structure of Uppark, for Repton was almost equally interested in
the interior decoration of his friend's house, and went to great
pains on his behalf. For instance, a letter dated January 5, 1812
mentioned a plan for the interior of the Gold and White Dining
Room, with a new arrangement for the display of plate on the
sideboards. Plaster plaques by Garrard were put up, and plaster
busts of Napoleon, Bedford, Charles James Fox and William
Battine, lawyer, poet and family friend, were placed in some
original oval decorations of Tankerville's era. The present dining
room chimney piece is attributed to Repton, who introduced
the mirrors at the four corners of the room, taking care to have
them set at an angle where the reflections are multiplied in
perspective. In connection with these mirrors, Repton wrote to
Sir Harry on July 6, 1812:

'You understand rightly—the opposite recesses to be the same
but without Looking Glasses—Your plan for the Glass is right—
but remember not to confine it too tight or it will break—put
lead or woollen cloth near the edges.'

Repton went to a great deal of trouble in connection with the
decorating of this particular room, as is shown by his letter of
October 6, 1813:

'I went first to Hancocks where I saw nothing but the old dish
pendant with two burners betwixt an wire reservoir. & the same
with one burner is unsymetrical—(anglise lop sided.)—& these
are all from 12 to 16 gns each—then I went to (I forget his
name) in Bond Street, the grand Luminary (again anglice lamp
man) of the Nation—He supplies Uppark with oil—the same
kind of lamps I found from 8 to 12 gns Why is this difference
betwixt *Tradesmen*—I believe 'em all rogues alike and only
differing in the *more* or the *less* here I saw a kind of lamp with
its reservoir under the burner and consequently avoiding the
Clumsy vase or Urn above. But when lighted—I found an
insuperable objection in the shadow cast from the opake
reservoir—this was attempted to be removed by a glass reservoir
—but there we see the oil. I then went to an ingenious
Lamponist not a Lampoonist — who invented those elegant

tripods which used last year to light Drury Lane Stage but have been laid aside this year because it was found to roast the Manager in his Box over it with this ingenious Monsr de Ville —(forsitan—devil).

'I had much conversation and it ended in his convincing me that oil could not be burnt without a reservoir, and that that must be visible and opake and in fact an ugly nuisance. he thought a large wax candle in an openwork socket and spring to keep the flame at a given height, would admit of a new design for which I have given him a sketch and he is to let me know the cost—this he says will be much less than either of the other plans and may correspond with the design I made for the cruet stand.'

Repton's mention of argand lights was a step from candlelight to the first oil lamps which would hide the oil that fed them. Repton constantly refers to this method of lighting and he expended time and thought on devising Regency stands for them which would conceal the source of the fuel supply. His letter continued:

'And now for the Plate Racks . . . at Wanstead House I saw the Plate decorated by a drapery of drap'd or embroidered but— c'estoit—l'or d'orre—(anglice buttered bacon) yet the drapery suggested the idea of a drapery of Garter Blue velvet with gold fringe which might be very magnificent in contrast to the Gold Plate and this led to considering how handsome the room might be if the yellow window curtains fell straight down the sides with the blue velvet drapery at the top—and at all events I would advise a blue velvet curtain for the painted window—I went to several Velvetaires and saw one piece which I could hardly believe to be of cotton so much did it resemble Genoese —but the difference of price is as 5/- to 36/- which amounts I think to this—"to be or not to be" only there is no question whether tis better etc etc.'

These ideas evidently did not attract Sir Harry. Perhaps the suggestions were too much in the style of the Prince Regent.

There was undoubtedly a hanging of some kind from the only brass curtain rail that exists at Uppark, over the Dining-Room door into the Serving Room. Repton and Sir Harry were to make a feature of a stained glass window which was to be erected on the north wall of this Serving Room.

Repton was busy with the window in January 1813 and he wrote:

'I was at Underwood's yesterday—and unpacked the Stained glass—of which I have only retained the circle as a center piece and we have adapted an entire new window—in which I first considered the effect of light and colour—both by day and candlelight for which reason the white ground glass forms the basis and the principle object will be a few figures in clear obscure on a white panel just the height of the eye—these will be taken from a pure classic model—as my son has made some sketches from the marbles imported from Athens by Lord Elgin. —of which there is a young man at Underwoods who can transfere the outlines on the white panel and by candlelight—the effect will be magic as all the light may proceed from this window from Argand Lamps properly adjusted from behind.'

In a postscript, he added:

'It is difficult by any drawing to give the effect of stained glass, the difference being as betwixt a thing opake—and translucent —but I have observed the white roughed glass gives most light with the blue but they give less light—and after making the sketch we thought we could improve the Circle—but I doubt it and have therefore sent both for your Decision.

'That intrellis supposes a little cut glass in the squares which by candlelight would be splendidly brilliant and is an object of no expense.

'At all events I think the dark blue large Circle should be orange for the sake of the increased light.'

In the same letter, he suggested:

'If you have a marble slab to spare perhaps we might support it on a mahogany frame for which my son has also given a hint in the same sketch which, if you should do him the honour to approve—need not be sent back for working drawings to be made for either or both having copies in our office and with or without the Cellaret under the slab—as you shall direct.'

This picture was not sent back to the office because Sir Harry did carry out the idea of marble slabs fitted into the recesses below the new mirrors.

Repton was a perfectionist and did not countenance false economies. He had stated these views very clearly in a letter of January 21, 1813:

'I have received the honour of your letter respecting the Looking glasses in the recesses—which I cannot make up my mind to answer—having never had so much knowledge of or respect for money as to hesitate between one thing or another on account of its cost unless I could not afford it—and then I did without— now I know your taste is so accurate that you would never forgive me if I could recommend a Glass with a crease across it in the room which you are in every respect fitting up in so elegant Style—yet the Times—sad times! require some deprivations and my advice should rather go to having two Glasses perfect, and put in blank panels opposite to try the effect—and if you cannot bear them, they may at any time be changed into Glasses—but I believe it is a true adage—"that a *Makeshift* is always bad economy"'—since it is better to do without the thing entirely— as you have very properly decided in the case of the Lampstand.'

The only other improvement we know that he made was installing the gold and white Regency book-cases along the north wall of the Saloon. He referred to these at the end of a letter written in November 1814:

'How you gratify my feelings by expressing your satisfaction with all we have done Are the bookcases done in the Salon— & will it be possible to use those at Simsons? It is a sore subject & I will say nothing of business . . . '

Business was one thing, public affairs another, and in 1814 Repton gave his friend and client some notion of the bustle in London due to the arrival of plenipotentiaries who had crossed the Channel as the result of Napoleon's first abdication and his banishment to Elba. Repton reported:

'I never saw the streets of London in such a fever of ferment— the streets all lined with military in New Uniforms—and filled with Carriages full of Ladies etc. etc. leaving a narrow lane for the traffic of those who "were kept moving"—but which I think must soon move *en masse*—I never saw such crowds—To see the hotel which contained these shoals of Emperors, Kings, Princes, Archduchesses etc.'

His humanity is revealed in the following description of the liberation of French prisoners of war:

'At Bath and Warminster I witnessed some curious scenes in the streets—each day three hundred had been liberated out of 8,400 prisoners in confinement near Bristol—and the joy and festivity of the poor devils contrasted with the doubts of others is not to be described—they went about singing and shaking hands with all they met and—delighted with children, of whom they had hardly seen any for many years—some very respectable looking men of good families dreaded returning to a country where they knew not if they had homes or relations—some had white cockades—but all spoke of Buonaparte as a great general though not fit to govern France . . . '

Sir Harry's letter of reply was evidently as cordial as ever, and it gave Repton the chance to offer a remarkable prophecy about the immediate future in France.

'The pleasure I ever feel in receiving a letter from you,' he wrote, 'was more than usual—because I suspected you had slipd off to the Coast & like many others of my Correspondents, were gone, to renew the pleasures of memory—which are too often dashed by regret (*to those who can regret anything*) I have conversed with many who have been to Paris & returned dissatisfied—nay almost disgusted—every thing is changed & from what I can gather—the Great Nation conquered is like a great Family reduced by misfortune—The Pride, the Gloriose Magnificence is ostentatiously displayed in the Splendour of Spectacle & old Finery while Poverty and Filth & sour discontent, rancle in the heart & they can neither resume the former Society of their Equals—nor condescend to mix with those who have risen from being their inferiors—& whose success like that of all *Nouveaux Gens* in all countries—is their only merit or object of thought.

'If you *really* must go to Paris—you must go soon—for those restless Monkeys, will be playing their tricks again—they begin to grow cool towards their natural enemies—& I should not wonder to find in a few months not only the Bourbons—but *tous les Anglais*—either kicked out of France or locked up in it—a Monkey is not to be trusted without a chain & the Allies left that of Frenchmen too long & too loose—they will snap it—Snap!'

On October 20, 1816, Repton gave Sir Harry an account of the bad harvest of that year:

'Plenty has vanished—and during my last two trips in Kent and Cambridgeshire I saw the fields, covered with Swathes and Sheaves of Corn more like the Straw of a Dung Yard than the fields of Harvest and we have hardly had a day of sunshine since—but I have no Corn fields to weep over—and a cloudy day seldom troubles me. Let me hope you amongst my friends are not a great sufferer and that you enjoy health and exercise as usual and that Uppark preserves its wonted beauty.'

Upstart war profiteers had invaded Repton's own village of Hare Street near Romford. In the letter of October he gave Sir Harry an account of them:

'I cannot see the ancient seats of our Nobility transferred to new men whose only claim is acquired wealth—perhaps fairly acquired—yet how seldom am I satisfied—as in the case of my friend Manning—that all is fair.

'In the vicinity of Hare Street we have many curious instances of Wealth in Strange hands—I will record four all recent cases within the present Year (No 1) a great Sugar baker doubles his Capital in a Day—buys Hare Hall and begins by stocking the 200 acres with 2 doz live Hares and half a dozen Squirrels—these he shuts up in his Walled Kitchen Garden from whence the latter hop off—and the former crop of all the Cauliflowers etc. (No. 2)—is a great Contractor for Tents and Bedding he lives in the Corner of Gidea Hall—doubles the rents of all the Cottages and Farms bought with the Estate — and they are all empty! The village of Hare Street desolate and depopulated—while the Literary Talents of the Natives are displayed in Vituperative Inscriptions chalked over all the Walls & Palings near him Curses not loud but deep from a once happy neighbourhood—(No 3) A Rich Banker has bought the Estate of a late Rich Grocer—& brings down to enliven his Sabbath days retirement—Mathews who is subject to low spirits & other celebrated wits whose good things are exchanged for the good thing which Wealth can purchase—& if it cannot purchase 'worshipful Society' then welcome 'Mendici, Mimae, Balatrones hos genus omne' Lastly comes (No 4) a neice fat fair and forty of an Uncle whose scraped up 60,000 £ *for She*—& left it all *to She* —as he said he would & now she gives it all to her Coachman & takes his Surname in return having dropd the Christian name with the reins—but he drives on like Jehu the Son of Nimshi who driveth furiously . . . '

Nothing is more eloquent of the fact that Repton found in Sir Harry a friend to whom he could unburden himself, long after their formal business was done, than those gossipy, inconsequential letters, and a series in which he told of the ups and downs—they were mostly downs—of his health. Repton loved Uppark for its own sake, 'improvements' apart, and in one of his letters, he anticipated the future, when he referred to the fact that 'the lawns and woods are open to the holiday visitors of rural felicity', adding that 'even the house itself throws open its doors to the inquisitive'.

Repton himself grew increasingly in a bad way, and in fact was only to survive until 1818. 'The business of my life,' he wrote, three years earlier:

'has been to prepare for others the enjoyments of the gifts of nature by adapting them to the use of man—and I have largely shared them with others—time now moves with heavy pace— the days linger—my limbs and my lungs refuse their office—my senses are becoming more blunt—and pain every hour brings me nearer to that change which must soon happen.'

On another occasion he confessed:

' . . . I have of late had very little to engage my attention professionally—unless I may reckon the painful necessity of discovering how difficult it is to settle any accounts with men without honour and I fear the honour of some people will not bear the test of necessity—honesty and poverty seldom go hand in hand . . . '

As for his physical infirmities, he wrote to Uppark in 1814 to say:

'I am just returned from Longleate where I was not able to walk an hundred yards without torture—I went to Bath—consulted Dr Parry—and rode about the streets in a three wheeled chair—I found my sentence pronounced by Sir Lachlan Maclane confirmed by Dr Parry—viz to reduce by diet—i.e. deprivation—and regimen i.e. depletion—to remove fat and give my blood room to pass through the large vessels—or submit to pain and death.

'There my dear Sir Harry, what becomes of my visit to France or even to Uppark, where I must die if I eat—and starve to keep alive but as fruit is not denied me I will come and enjoy your fruit in spite of the fruits of good living—but here again new difficulties occur—I that used to travel 5 thousand miles in a year without a farthing expense—now cannot move fifty without prudence teling me I ought to be satisfied with former journeys so I will stay at home and write when tired of reading —*Ecce Signum*.

'On the concurrence of opinion — of Dr MacLean and Dr Parry.

Says Death to the Devil—in family chat
Surely Repton is now grown sufficiently fat
His heart is þrimful and his veins are all filled
And soon you'll pronounce it is time he were killed
Very true, says the Devil, in that I agree
But I doubt his belonging to you or to me,
Since two Drs agree one opinion to give
He must leave off good living the longer to live.
Thus MacLean and Parry—Parry devil and death
They make lean our quarry and give him new breath
And then after all—should Death's Dart chance to hit
Little share you will have of him—nor the Devil a bit.—

Thus will I trifle away betwixt the intervals of pain enjoying pleasure and as you say we are nearly of the same age—if my sheet were not so full I should be tempted to send you my reflections on Sexaginosity—appropos These Royal and Imperial and Archducal Lions are to go to hear the British Lion roar at Spithead—how I wish I could sail to Uppark in a baloon and bring you a New telescope . . . '

Did Sir Harry watch this review from his father's wooden gothic shelter?

In November of the same year, Repton wrote again to Sir Harry:

'In a few words I will tell you that a disease which has for years been gradually alarming me by spasms in my Chest—has of late taken the decided symtoms of Angina Pectoris—a difficulty in the transmition of blood from some obstruction in the Larger vessels of the Heart—attended by the most painful spasms after standing—or walking uphill or upstairs—while on Level ground or in a Carriage—or at my desk—I am well as ever, easy in body and happy in mind—then what reason have I to complain but consider—it has been the constant habit of my last fifty years to walk from 10 to 20 miles a day—to search for beauty, or to make it in places difficult of access—& to make that access easy to others now I cannot walk ten yards & am obliged to be carried in a Chair like Guy Faux on the 5th Nov. or walk like Asmodeur with two sticks. Yet I do not shrink from business—& tho I have not been within 50 miles of Uppark—I have been twice in Norfolk—& once in Devonshire & after being retained 2 months in Norfolk by an accident which happened to Mrs Repton I am once more returned to Essex, & have set myself a Task which must call forth all the execution of which I am yet capable—I am collecting my material for another volume of Landscape Gardening—I had in some sort arranged many for a posthumous work—but if a man can publish his thought while he is alive—it is better than speaking from the Grave, so I am very *gravely* thankful that such an opportunity of *living a little longer* seems to be granted me—& tho I did not expect to live to come back into Essex—& actually made a purchase of a little snug corner in Aylsham Church yard—with an intent to have my Mold converted into a bed of roses—& my grave a flower garden—yet I am content to revise the gardens I have made & Live a little longer —Aye & who knows but we may meet at Uppark if not at Paris by avoiding Exercise and Eating—I am certainly better —but it is the Nature of the desease to be incurable—& suddenly fatal. I therefore when I first went to Aylsham—concluded that my spasms would soon conclude my business—Mrs. Repton's fall downstairs—raised me from falling into my Grave but during the time I daily expected it—I never enjoyed life more than when I used to indulge in planning a small flower garden for the purpose and every day I wrote something on the spot—such trifles as this—e.g.

Three barley corns one inch, we are told—nine inches make
one span
Thus at our fingers ends we hold, the boasted life of Man.
Then what avails the Fear of Death, Or what life's greatest
pleasure?
Since shortly we resign our breath; Submitting to Short
measure.
Acres and Miles I've pac'd around, to make my gardens grow
But now within this hallow'd, three paces are enow.'

Courageously the sick man ignored his weaknesses. On 21 August 1815, he recorded:

'I resolved to sink the invalid & try the experiment of Devon Air—I have been to Tavistock to meet the Duke of Bedford—& returned last night so much the better for my journey that I am strongly tempted by the kind and Cordial proposal you hold out —to pass a week at Uppark before the summer air has taken leave of its Lawns—or the Summer flowers its Gardens & perhaps before the Autumn fruits have begun their wonted blushes —in short if I knew in what part of next month—September— my visit would least clash with your arrangements—I should run down without considering—Air, or Flowers or Fruits for the Satisfaction of passing three or four days in that society from which I have so often derived amusement and instruction—This is the first visit I ever felt inclined to make independent of all professional pursuit—& now it is time to think of enjoying the Scenes I have created—while any powers of enjoyment remain— I know you will let me do as I please, or rather as I can—& I will bring with me as my *Guarde Malade* & support—that son whose pencil has been rendered useful to Uppark—to him a few days of vacation will be peculiarly acceptable—and of these he will will be glad to pass one in fishing for Pike — his only field sport—.'

This visit was evidently a great success. In October of the same year Repton wrote, apologising for allowing a month to pass without thanking Sir Harry 'for that week of perfect

enjoyment' and claiming that it had so far benefited his health
that he had been able:

'to make a short professional trip in the same direction though
only half way in point of distance—I have been giving my
opinion respecting a spot—with relation to a future residence
in one of the very few beautiful scenes, which a high-road com-
mands—it is at Mickleham—in that vale of the blind and sleepy
and fanciful River Mole—betwixt Leatherhead and Dorking—I
know of no such scenery anywhere *visible* to the public—for it
is now a melancholy truth that every proprietor possessed of
land near a high-road begins his improvement by excluding the
world, and shutting up himself in his place within an im-
penetrable screen of pailing and planting, miserable consequence
of ownership—he delights in calling it his own and proving it
is so—by excluding everyone else.'

In the following year he also paid visits to some of the scenes
of his former triumphs but admitted that much as he wished to
travel to Uppark, 'alas! my poor heart pants at the idea and I
dread coming to a Rupture with my bosom friend.'

Sir Harry sent his friend generous presents of 'gibier' to
support his failing health. So constant were Sir Harry's attentions that Repton wrote in January 1816:

'In my Letters to Sir Harry Featherstone—the same form of
thanks for favors received—so often occurs, that it would be
better to have a printed form, like the Cards which are attached
to our beautiful Envoys and which by seeing your handwriting
—lead me to hope you are as well as usual—but you ought to
be better than usual—if our Libations have any efficacy—since
not a week has passed since the shooting season came in—but
we have had occasion to commemorate the Donor of a Dainty
at our Table—

'Often I have wish'd to know how I could send you an
Elephant—as the word *Equivalent* was once spelt— . . . One
day while puzzling over this difficult subject of Compensations
—I received from a friend a Case containing about a hundred
volume of Modern french books neatly bound—with a request
that I would take charge of them for 3 or 4 months—it immediately occurd to me that I could send you a score vol.s at a time,

and thus make an exchange of food for mind & food for body—
& asked my friend leave to make such use of his Depot—.'

Repton shared with Sir Harry an interest in reading,
especially French books. 'What are you now reading?' he asked
on May 30, 1815. 'Have you any good light french reading like
August la Fontaine's *Aline*? This fills up gaps of life for without
power of Loco Motion such gaps will occur . . . ' In the following January, he commented favourably on *Guy Mannering* and
Helen Maria Williams' *Present State of France*, but at the same
time he remarked on 'this Cold Weather when the glossy
binding makes one's fingers ache'.

With the realism which characterised his attitude towards
death, he frequently referred to his approaching end. He ended
his letter dater 2nd January 1816 thus:

'One has 363 days to look forward to without much hope except
that they may lead to some more satisfactory & permanent
system of existence—since this is so empty & fugitive but such
Comments are all Fudge—Ehu fugares! But whether here or
elsewhere believe me Most Cordially

Yours H.R.'

His condition remained fluctuating, and a year later he wrote:

' . . . I am sure you will be pleased to hear that my health is
so much improved that I forget my . . . chair-stick and my
harpoon and I sally forth till I can . . . go no further, but
instead of 20 yards I can go 200 and I often think were I now
at Uppark—I could reach my bedroom without resting on the
Landing — O *Rus quando te aspician! Quando que videbo
Upparkias tuas!*' . . .

In a letter to Sir Harry of 8th October, 1815, Repton wrote
the following:

'I felt in the service of this day—most peculiarly those words of
David "Lord, let me know my end and the number of my days
that I may be certified how long I have to live" . . . for some
time past, I have uniformly awaked a few minutes before the
Twilight & the watching its gradual progress, has sometimes
made a Diversion in my pain, while I seem to struggle with the
Coming Day—in one of these contentions I (as usual) penciled
out my thoughts— . . .

TWILIGHT

The Twilight dawns, another day's beginning
Thus while we sleep, this Whirligig keeps spinning
E'en in the dark, the thread of life is spun
And now—another motley day's begun.
We little know the texture of this thread
Whether as Cobweb weak, or Cart rope strong
Nor will I rack my brain, or Crack my head
In finding out life's thread—how short, how long.
Enough for me to know when each is past
That every Spasm had nearly been my last
While every Day 'twixt intervals of pain
Reverberates with hope to live again
Then welcome Dawn—welcome Aurora's Ray
Welcome bright Harbinger of future Day.'

A design for a french sconce.

V

Marriage to a Dairy-Maid

Waterloo, and the final ending to the long war, found Sir Harry in an uncertain state of mind. He had made his improvements, but he was a man of over sixty with no heir, and not much prospect of one. In one of the very last letters of his life, Repton had enquired:

'Now let me ask how it moves with you—perhaps I am writing to Uppark while you are in a distant part of Europe—for surely you will not let another summer pass without taking advantage of visiting the Continent before the Archfiend returns to stop you.'

Sir Harry in fact acted with none of the haste which had caused his journey in 1802. Perhaps he felt that Repton was right, and that Napoleon would return, even from distant St Helena, once more to disturb the peace of Europe. He waited three full years before his next visit to Paris.

Meanwhile, he actually seems to have entertained thoughts of selling Uppark, and the wish of the nation to present Wellington with a country estate in token of their admiration for his magnificent services in the war just finished, opened up a possible opportunity to dispose of the estate to advantage.

The Duchess of Richmond had written from Cambrai inquiring if Stansted or Idsworth would be available, to which Sir Harry replied:

'I really see nothing for it unless I make over Uppark to the Duke and retire to a warm climate, as every old batchelor should at my time of life . . . Your absence makes a great gap in the Country and regretted by no one more sincerely than myself.'

The Duke of Wellington, corresponding with the Duchess of Richmond, had this to say:
'According to what I have heard of Uppark I don't know of any

place that would suit me so well . . . I feel rather prejudiced in favour of that County . . . '

In June 1816, the Duke sent Benjamin Wyatt to see Sir Harry, but by that time Sir Harry may have felt he had been too precipitate in suggesting Uppark as a suitable choice, and the hesitation he now felt made him write to the Duchess saying that the 'proposition with regard to Uppark was not *meant* to be altogether so serious'.

The Duke had agreed to the conditions suggested for thirty years' purchase for the estate upon a new valuation of the Farms, as well as the valuation of the park and timber, and noted that Sir Harry required a price for the house.

When it became obvious to Sir Harry that the Duke intended demolishing the house he wrote:

' . . . if I had been aware of Your Grace's intentions to execute the plan of one from the ground, I really should not have ventured to mention Uppark at all, being perfectly sensible that the sum I might name (and I have no hesitation in saying it cannot be a small one) for the House and Offices in their present state . . . would admit of additions corresponding to the scale required . . . and therefore may partially weigh against the eligibility of the purchase both in Your Grace's opinion and that of the Trustees . . . '

The sum he mentioned in a later letter was £90,000 for the house alone.

The following August the Duke wrote:

' . . . that it is quite clear to me that even if you should be desirous to sell Uppark at the time you had fixed . . . it will be impossible for me to be the purchaser. I will therefore give you no further trouble on the subject.'

The Duke had in fact come down to see Uppark for himself. The steepness of the hill and drive seemed a formidable obstacle. 'I have crossed the Alps once,' he is said to have exclaimed, and promptly drove home. He estimated he would have to buy new horses every eighteen months!

Sir Harry's visit to Paris in 1819 resulted in a long letter to his old friend Arthur Paget, now a Marquess and one of the heroes of Waterloo, where he had lost a leg.

' . . . Paris has not lost its ground with me on this second visit,' so he wrote, 'and I am still satisfied it will be a grand desideratum for a *part* of the year. The exposition of all the works of art and manufacturers of France at the Louvre is truly wonderful: it has been open now above a month and closes on Friday, the King [Louis XVIII] having already distributed the prize medals (many hundreds) in person and said something flattering to the different artists for which, I understand, he has a very happy *tournure*. From the most costly bouquets of diamonds to the humble efforts of the blind there is such an endless variety of objects of all classes, no words can describe it. One thing however is demonstrated; such industry applied to the great resources of this Country will soon wipe away old scores. She will be a Giant refreshed. I am much amused in my morning walks, and for the rest of the day till dinner it is only an *embarras* of choice; the two Operas on alternate nights close the evening, and to anyone who loves Italian Musick, the *Theatre Royal Italian* offers at this moment prodigious allurement, for such a *Company together* has seldom met; Pellegrini is inimitable and the Fodor in high force. The ballets at the Grand Opera are of *course* perfection. Last Monday I dined with Sheldon; a dinner *très récherché* and *really* well dressed, his Sillery excellent; besides the Ladies of his family were the Ducs D'Escar and D'Aumont (the latter well known to me formerly), the Counts D'Escar and La Ferronays (Lately appointed to Petersburgh), and Sir Charles Stuart [British Ambassador]: altogether a very pleasant dinner. The old Duc D'Escar is to give us one at the Tuilleries next week, and I am told I shall see the *best going,* but he acknowledged to me that there were no *Chefs now* equal to some before the Revolution, which justifies my opinion. I never saw anyone young or old eat so much with *Melon* in the middle of it all. Talk of stomach indeed! I am a very poor creature.'

France was so refreshing to his spirit that Sir Harry continued:

'I have seen several things in the environs of Paris to be sold, and one belonging to the Duchess de Feitre, which I like much;

but I shall not decide hastily about it and in the meantime am
in treaty with the Princess de Chimay (formerly Madame
Tallien) for her Hotel next Spring. It is a delightful thing with
7 acres of pleasure ground *in* Paris. She very politely showed me
over the whole herself, and I was very glad to come in contact
with so celebrated a person, who is still handsome and very
pleasant in her manner. She is a little exorbitant just now, but
as Princesses often lower their terms, I think it is very likely I
shall have it, as she has promised her ultimatum soon . . . '

The idea came to nothing, though Sir Harry paid one more
visit to France in 1824, when he was seventy. By that time he
had made friends with Charles Heathcote Tatham, an architect,
artist and collector who had designed the decorations for Drury
Lane Theatre. Tatham was gay, amusing, often irreverent and
sometimes blasphemous. Sketches made on visits to friends and
patrons included several scenes at Uppark. One such sketch
depicted the Archbishop of York playing billiards with Lady
Carlisle on a miniature table. A similar table was introduced by
Tatham to Uppark, preceding the larger billiard tables. His
talent suited Sir Harry's declining years, who vowed he would
remember Tatham in his Will, but afterwards revoked it.

Tatham drew plans for further alterations to Uppark. A long
room with three windows was to have been built above Repton's
Portico. An Entrance Hall was planned; the staircase was to have
been moved and a gallery on pillasters was to circle the Hall.
But the plans never materialized, and Tatham rode away one
day on a galloping horse, never to return: a final departure
which, with a flourish, he illustrated himself. Once more Sir
Harry was back on his own resources.

The companionship of his friends and neighbours was not
enough. He was restless and unhappy and spent hours pacing
the garden or riding wildly through the village. Immediately
to the west of the house is a sheltered lawn, which was the old
Bowling Green in the days of Lord Tankerville. Along the
north side there is a grass banked terrace that extends along the
front of the red brick stable buildings and adjoining walls, ending
in Repton's little shelter, with its four slender white pillars
supporting the curved white roof. Here, on the white slatted
seats, Sir Harry could entertain his guests with Devonshire

cream made in the cool dairy behind the door. The tiled dairy
had windows of Regency glass, blue, orange and white. White
tiles with a border of blue convolvulus made a pretty setting
for the large bowls and earthenware crocks on the marble tables
full of Guernsey cream and milk, furnished by the Uppark herd.

One day, as Sir Harry sauntered on the grass terrace, he
caught the sound of a girl's voice singing. He asked the Housekeeper who was the girl whose voice had attracted him so much.
'Not the Dairymaid, Sir Harry, she be too old—', was the
reply. Sir Harry continued to listen to the voice that charmed
him. The Dairymaid had helpers; one day, when the noise of
angry voices was heard as he approached the Dairy, he heard a
girl's voice saying, 'Peace, peace . . . '; and there was peace.
The old Dairymaid retired, and the girl who cried 'Peace,
peace . . . ' was established as head of the Dairy with a hand-
ful of girls at her command. Her name was Mary Ann Bullock.

Sir Harry continued to visit the shelter and enjoy the view
of the Downs over the curved laurel hedge which Repton had
introduced to border the lawn below the terrace. From the Dairy
shelter one of the most pleasing views of the house can be seen.
One day, Sir Harry presented himself at the door of the Dairy.
He told Mary Ann he wanted to marry her.

In an account, never to be forgotten, of the episode told by a
later Dairymaid who had heard the story from contemporaries,
Mary Ann was said to be speechless; 'taken aback like . . . '.
'Don't answer me now,' said Sir Harry, 'but if you will have
me, cut a slice out of the leg of Mutton that is coming up for
my dinner today . . . ' When the Mutton arrived, the slice
was cut. Contemporary stories dwell long and lovingly on the
rage and surprise of the Cook. Surprise was heard on all sides.
'I hear Sir Harry Fetherston is to marry his cook,' wrote Mrs
Arbuthnot to the Duke of Wellington.

The romance of the Milkmaid took many aback. Having
decided to marry Mary Ann, Sir Harry set about her education.
She was sent to Paris. There she learnt to read and write a very
good hand; she embroidered in wool, and her work is easily
recognised, for her taste was highly conventional.

Pious and gentle Miss Sutherland, then aged nineteen, with
whose mother Sir Harry had once diverted his time, lived under
her father's protection at Uppark. She was one of the witnesses

to his marriage in the Saloon on 12th September, 1825. Sir Harry was seventy-one; Mary Ann was twenty. The Rector did not officiate, and they were married by the Vicar of Harting, Mr. Cookson, who had ministered in the parish for nearly thirty years.

Sir Harry bought a string of pearls for his wife. Receipts for other jewellery, of a strictly Victorian character also survive. There was some exchange of plate, and the Tenier-patterned Tea Urn and teapots *en appanage*, all of heavy respectability, made their appearance.

The couple used to go driving in the Park, and one day a little girl opened a gate for them and threw a bunch of flowers into her lap. 'We will have her at Uppark and educate her,' said Sir Harry, when he heard the little girl was Mary Ann's sister. In educating Frances Bullock, there was an additional object in his mind. His daughter, Miss Sutherland, would have employment and interest in teaching his small sister-in-law: in fact, she remained her friend and companion to the end of her life.

That Mary Ann's position was not always enviable was shown on another occasion. Sir Harry and his Lady drove up to the Portico and the footman waiting to receive them laughed at the former Dairymaid. Sir Harry, in a rage, dismissed him on the spot, but he could not dismiss the titters that went round Society circles, nor could he induce the County to accept his wife. At times he evidently doubted his own commonsense. Soon after his marriage, he unburdened himself to the old Uppark gamekeeper, saying: 'I've made a fool of myself, Legge'.

The new Lady Fetherstonhaugh was in fact kindly, devoted and industrious, and Sir Harry could have done a great deal worse. At that time, German dyes were beginning to cause wonder and attention. Mary Ann's needlework which was for the most part faithful imitations of patterns she brought back from Paris. She executed some remarkable work raised on duvteen, which she spread on a Chippendale chair in the stone Hall. Perhaps Sir Harry did not like it, for there is only one example. Otherwise, firescreens and innumerable footstools, occupied her attention.

Sir Harry and his wife established the school in Harting village. It was built at Sir Harry's expense on its present site, which had to be freed from the occupation of one of his tenants, who proved refactory and obstinate.

The time soon came when Sir Harry's own figure rivalled the corpulency he had once mocked in the Prince Regent. There are back-rests and wheeled chairs to show Mary Ann's care of her husband in the last decades of his life. His Bedroom was the Tapestry Room. His big wooden bath could be wheeled into the Lobby, where water was laid on, and a cosy fire burnt coal which was handled and carried by innumerable attendants for all the fireplaces in the house. A picture of 'poor Napoleon' hung over the mirror opposite Sir Harry's four-poster bed, but even the Napoleonic Wars had brought relatively little change to the mode of life at Uppark.

The question of his Arms and pedigree interested Sir Harry as much as it had done his father. Heraldically, the Fether-stonhaugh arms were 'Gules on a Chevron between Three Ostrich feathers Argent a Black roundle, with an escutcheon of Ulster'. Sir Harry kept many papers on the subject, and deputed Mr. Boustead, his secretary, to enter into the necessary negotia-tions with the College of Heralds for the registration of the Arms of Mary Ann Bullock in an appropriate manner so that they might be quartered with his own. On 14th June 1848, he wrote to Mr. Boustead:

'My Dear Sir,

In acknowledging the receipt of your last letter, I beg to enclose for the signature of Lady Fetherston the usual Memorial to the Earl Marshall for the registration of the Arms of Bullock, and request that you will have the goodness to return it to me when signed . . . '

Hatchments in the nave of South Harting church show the Fetherstonhaugh and Bullock arms together.

Sir Harry died at Uppark, at the age of ninety-two, on October 24, 1846. He left everything he possessed to his wife. The span of his life, with that of his wife who died in 1875 and his sister-in-law who survived until 1895, covered 141 years, and brought Uppark through the Victorian era practically untouched.

Sir Harry's body lay coffined in the chancel of Harting Church for a whole year. During that time the chancel arch was parti-tioned off, and services were held in the nave. It had been decided to bury him in the Tankerville vault but the wall was so roughly done that older coffins were thrown aside and broken. Some of the plates were placed in the arch of the tomb which is the resting place of Sir Edward Ford the cavalier. It was at this time of alteration and disturbance that Ford, Lord Grey of Werke and Earl of Tankerville, was discovered with his Dutch pipe.

VI

Victorian Afternoon

After her husband's death, Lady Fetherstonhaugh, still in the prime of life, settled down to the long Victorian afternoon, varying her country routine with occasional visits to London. She restored Harting Church, putting in four lancet windows of Victorian glass above the altar, and erecting a stone memorial tablet on the north wall below to the last Fetherstonhaugh squire of Harting Manor. A lone figure of grief below a sheltered oak symbolised the rectitude of one who described herself as Sir Harry's 'devoted and grateful widow'. Richard Westmacott, designer of this marble, even remembered to insert a faithful dog. During the alterations to the church Miss Sutherland undertook the carving of the capitals of the pillars for the font, and this she did under the direction of a stone-carver at Brighton.

Mary Ann Fetherstonhaugh's was not an original mind, for which posterity may be thankful, for she could have created havoc in the old house, or even sold it. She lived to continue its traditions, and if she was not favoured by Society, she could at least exercise thought for those around her. At Christmas time, tables of gifts were spread in the Great Hall, and within living memory, descriptions of the piles of red flannel petticoats and mounds of red rounds of beef and Christmas pies and puddings have been lovingly retailed. Thirty years ago, there still remained a few who had seen these things, people with memories of Mary Ann's generosity.

Both Lady Fetherstonhaugh and her sister managed their retinue of servants by fair and just rule. 'It is a very good thing,' commented Mary Ann, 'to be a Downstairs person as well as an Upstairs person,' when she convicted the head Gamekeeper of drunkenness. The man was dismissed, but the day's sport continued under another authority, and the guns returned to find the plates of oysters waiting for them on the marble console tables of the Stone Hall. Young Mrs Scrase Dickens was considered rather fast. She joined the gentlemen uninvited at their oyster feasts, when her husband was one of the guns. It should be added in fairness to this lady, that she was one of those who befriended and valued the Dairymaid.

Among well known servants at Uppark were Bucky Loton, the Head Cleaver of Deerpark fences, who was photographed in his white round smock with a group of his friends: Jumper Chitty, who walked to Midhurst Calvinist Church every Sunday, and Wargy Watts, with white wands of willow, talismans of the Harting Old Club. All drank the home-brewed beer, and all cleaned the silver plates with sand and straw in the old Great Hall after a big dinner party in the Gold and White Dining Room, and the Paul Storr dishes with the twined snake handles. The footmen wore large buttonholes edged with maidenhair fern. Miss Fetherston could never make out why people had trouble with their footman's names: she called one 'Hedward', and the other ''Enry', no matter what their names were. It saved confusion. No wonder those who knew her described her as 'of great character'. The Queen Anne silver bowl which was used when Sir Harry was christened in the Saloon, was used by Miss Fetherston to wash her hands in her bedroom.

One of the upper servants, Joseph Weaver, had a special place in the household from the first, and made life a great deal easier for Mary Ann than it would otherwise have been. Weaver had been engaged before Sir Harry's marriage. He had originally been in service with Arthur Paget, Sir Harry's closest friend, and in a letter writter to Paget in 1811, when he was about to engage him, the prospective employer said:

'Pray caution Mr Weaver to keep his wages to himself as so much exceeding those of my *old* servants.'

When Weaver was once installed, Sir Harry became enthusiastic. He wrote to Paget:

'Weaver came last Wednesday, and I am much prepossessed in his favour by his manner, and particularly by the graceful way in which he speaks of yourself. I auger well from this beginning and have no doubt of his making me a valuable servant . . .

would to God I had not so woefully experienced the PER CONTRA.'

Sir Harry was right in his judgment. Weaver lived to be the oracle of Uppark, and a son of the same name, who lived until 1885 was also a pillar of the household and a particular favourite with his master. Both were ardent natural historians, and many existing glass cases testify to their abilities as taxidermists. The Weavers not only collected shells, but their arrangements in the Chinese Cabinet show an artistic skill and a delicacy of touch in keeping with their characters. The younger Weaver acted as agent and secretary to Lady Fetherstonhaugh and later to her sister, and became in due time responsible for the memorial to his patroness in Harting Church, where there is a plaque to his own memory. The commemorative west window shows a series of acts of charity such as Mary Ann was accustomed to perform. She died in January 1874 leaving Weaver a 'handsome legacy', which, she stated:

'I wish him to understand is a reward for his grateful attention to Sir Harry . . . ' who 'would have made a more ample provision for him then than he did, had circumstances permitted. Sir Harry expressly commended him to my consideration, and I have, as you know, found him of very great assistance to me for the last seventeen years, during all which time his services have been given gratuitously.'

Lady Fetherstonhaugh made her will with her customary shrewdness. In a letter written to her sister she stated:

'To avoid encumbering my Will with unnecessary details, I have made no mention of William, Frederick, Joseph, Mrs Lover or Maria, because experience has led me to believe that neither of them is capable of taking care of large sums of money.'

She therefore left them all annuities, to be administered by her sister, which would be 'out of their power to squander away'. But 'Louisa', who was 'provident and will take care of what I leave her', was given her portion in a lump sum.

Frances Bullock adopted the name of Fetherstonhaugh on the death of her sister and the arms granted to Mary Ann were assigned to her. Together, Miss Sutherland and Miss

Fetherstonhaugh, the two old ladies of Uppark, came to have a legendary quality as they lived their quiet lives in the old house, where their one great wish was to ''ave everything as Sir 'Arry 'ad it . . . '.

Miss Fetherstonhaugh in due time sent for a maid she had once employed to become housekeeper at Uppark. This maid had married one of the former garden staff, and their son, H. G. Wells, later to become celebrated as a writer, recorded in his *Experiment in Autobiography* [1]

'My mother became housekeeper at Uppark in 1880 . . . During her thirteen years' sway . . . and thanks largely to the reliefs and opportunities that came to me through that brief interval of good fortune in her life, I had been able to do all sorts of things.'

He related how on one occasion when he was at Uppark:

'a great snow-storm snowed me up for nearly a fortnight, and I produced a daily newspaper of a facetious character—*The Uppark Alarmist*—on what was properly kitchen paper—and gave a shadow play to the maids and others, in a miniature theatre I had made in the Housekeeper's room . . . '

He acknowledged that:

'the place had a great effect on me; it retained a vitality that altogether overshadowed the ebbing tide of upstairs life, the two elderly ladies in the parlour following their shrunken routines . . . '

In a striking passage, Wells summarised all that Uppark and its inhabitants stood for:

' . . . it is one of my firmest convictions,' he wrote, 'that modern civilisation was begotten and nursed in the households of the prosperous, relatively independent people, the minor nobility, the gentry and the larger bourgeoise, which became visibly important in the landscape of the sixteenth century, introducing a new architectural element in the towns, and spreading as country houses and chateaux and villas over the continually more ordered countryside. Within these households,

[1] H. G. Wells' *Experiment in Autobiography*, London, Gollancz, 1934.

behind their screen of deer park and park wall and sheltered service, men could talk, think and write at their leisure. They were free from inspection and immediate imperatives . . . They went on the Grand Tour to see and learn.'

No doubt with the Fetherstonhaughs in mind, Wells warmed to his theme.

'They could be interested in public affairs without being consumed by them. The management of their estates kept them in touch with reality without making exhausting demands on their time. Many, no doubt, degenerated into a life of easy dignity or gentlemanly vice, but quite a sufficient number remained curious and interested to make, foster and protect the accumulating science and literature of the seventeenth and eighteenth centuries. Their large rooms, their libraries, their collections of pictures and 'curios' retained into the nineteenth century an atmosphere of unhurried liberal enquiry; of serene and determined insubordination and personal dignity, of established aesthetic and intellectual standards. Out of such houses came the Royal Society . . . the first museums and laboratories and picture galleries, gentle manners, good writing and nearly all that is worth while in our civilisation today. Their culture, like the culture of the ancient world, rested on a toiling class. Nobody bothered very much about that, but it has been far more through the curiosity of and enterprise and free deliberate thinking of these independent gentlemen than through any other influences, that modern machinery and economic organisation have developed so as to abolish at last the harsh necessity for any toiling class whatever.'

This is one of the most remarkable tributes ever paid to the spirit of Uppark and of houses like it, and it came from a man more familiar with the ways of the backstairs than of the grander rooms. Wells painted a portrait of Uppark in his novel *Tono-Bungay* (1909) in which it appears as 'Bladsover' and where some of the intricacies of the servants' hierarchy are amusingly sketched.

Miss Fetherstonhaugh sustained the life of the household on the pattern set by her sister almost throughout the reign of Victoria. It was a paradisical era for her servants, and it was small wonder that they sometimes got out of hand, one of them driving her full tilt into a field of standing corn, when he had had more to drink than was good for him. She and her companion always wore black velvet, as they thought it suited the house, but Miss Fetherstonhaugh, so it was remembered, 'liked something red in her hat when she went out'.

The shooting parties continued, and the house was sometimes lent to friends for their honeymoon. Lord and Lady Winterton were so favoured, and so were Lord and Lady Leconfield. As the Leconfield carriage reached the final hill before Uppark, Lord Leconfield discovered that the postilion was drunk, and rated him in no meek terms. As he handed his bride out of the coach he said: 'I regret that your ears heard that which they were never made to hear!' Other friends of standing were Lord and Lady Clanwilliam, who had settled at Stanstead, a pretty drive over the Downs.

As Miss Fetherstonhaugh grew old, speculation increased as to her choice of an heir. She kept her secret until the very end of her life. Sir Harry had shown less interest in his relations than they had in him, but Miss Fetherstonhaugh made lengthy and conscientious attempts, through her lawyers, to establish some relationship with the Northumbrian family. In the end she became satisfied that she would do no harm to her conscience by making an independent choice.

Miss Sutherland died at a great age in August 1893, and for nearly two years Miss Fetherstonhaugh lived alone. She died in June 1895, having made up her mind that house and estate, well preserved as they were, needed a man at the helm. She and her sister are buried in a small enclosure in Harting churchyard, and in her will she left the Uppark property to her friend Colonel the Hon Keith Turnour, brother of the Lord Winterton whose parents had honeymooned in the house. Colonel Turnour assumed the name and was granted the arms of Fetherstonhaugh, and lived for thirty-five years to enjoy his good fortune. One of his few and most sensible innovations was to abandon the old kitchen quarters and the elaborate tunnels by which meals were brought to the house, and to make new dispositions in the basement of the house itself. The old kitchens remain a feature fascinating to the visitor, eloquent testimony to days when labour was a plentiful commodity, and a complete little world of their own. As Colonel Turnour's son predeceased Miss Fetherstonhaugh, she had had to consider someone to follow after his life tenancy, the succession being designated to a second son.

In due time, the heir became the Hon Herbert Meade, son of Admiral of the Fleet the Earl of Clanwilliam, a favourite friend of the ladies of Uppark. Like his father, Herbert was in the navy, and he also reached flag rank, after a career of high distinction. Admiral Sir Herbert Meade-Fetherstonhaugh and his family have lived at Uppark for over thirty years, and their care has been to conserve its beauty and to hand it on.

By one of those chances which seem more than mere coincidence, when the new owners opened Miss Fetherstonhaugh's visitors book, which they found on a table in the Saloon, they discovered that the last entries made during her lifetime were those of the Admiral's parents.

Epilogue

by Margaret Meade-Fetherstonhaugh

Sometimes we would leave the salty tang of Portsmouth
Dockyard, where ships and men prepared for the life-and-death
struggle of the First World War. We would drive to the Sussex
Downland, where peace and beauty lived in that tumbled
countryside.

A lane runs halfway up the side of a Down, where yews and
junipers grow that were planted by the Romans. We stopped at
a gap in a hedgerow of beech and thorn to see suddenly the
view of Uppark, a house that was one day to be our home. It
was always a breath-taking experience. Uppark stands like some
rose-coloured altar among columned beech trees set into the
summit of the Downs.

We returned to the world of men and ships, white ensigns
that swept the seas, and anchor cables that sounded arrivals, or
'hail and farewell'. Before the sailor was to come into his own at
Uppark he fought destroyers and light cruisers in all engage-
ments in the North Sea, and on dark night patrols. He was later
to sail the world in the *Renown*, when he took the Prince of
Wales to India, and he was to command destroyer flotillas in
the Mediterranean, and work on Naval Staffs.

He had taken me to stay at Uppark soon after we married.
The marked kindness of our reception was the foundation of
many happy visits to Colonel Keith Turnour Fetherstonhaugh
and his daughter.

A racing Metalurgique brought us to the stone-pillared
portice of Uppark one autumn day, when the beeches had
turned lemon and gold against cloudless blue skies. On such a
day Uppark held heraldic splendour over the green park, where
herds of fallow deer grazed, and bracken brakes were red and
gold. Among my first impressions colour and light shone in an
unbroken tranquillity of peace, which impressed and held one.

No house I had ever seen was so filled with treasures of

Chippendale and china, of ormolu and Buhl, Chinese cabinets and Chinese vases jostling one another on floors and tables, with a thousand objects of peculiar personal character belonging to the memories of those intimately connected with Uppark for over three hundred years.

Tea was served majestically by the old butler from Teniers tea-urns on magnificent salvers, and at dinner elaborate entrée dishes of Lamerie and Paul Storr accompanied the silver plates, so when my French maid exclaimed next morning with excited eagerness: 'Mais, Madame, dans la Housekeeper's room c'est tout en argent!' I was not surprised. She had a connoisseur's eye and was never mistaken. As she placed the gleaming brass water-can inside the Dresden china basin, painted with Meissen jonquils and roses, on the washstand, I wondered how to leave a bed from which one opened wide eyes on eighteen miles of sunlit country to the sea.

But like the troubadours who kept the singing roses in their hearts during their wanderings, I said farewell to the tricolour convolvulus and briar-roses that covered the hand-printed wall-papers of my room at Uppark, and followed the calls of the sea, which led us in and out of twenty houses in twenty years in England, Scotland and Malta, until the time came to enter into the fairy story of our lives at Uppark.

In these days, when anyone can press a button and work magic, there are people who think that wonder is reprehensible weakness, and that magic should be controlled. If you make up your mind to mistrust wonder you will never know the fun of adventure.

Some might say: 'Fortune brought us here'; others, even more careful about keeping imagination suppressed, would say: 'Circumstances brought about a change in our environment', which is really the same way of putting it without any lift to the imagination.

It was February 1931 when we came to live at Uppark, driving over the Surrey hills, round the Devil's Punch Bowl, till we came through the village of Harting and, climbing the steep hill, stopped before the house.

Our adventure had begun.

Harry Fetherstonhaugh looked down from over the Saloon door in the hall and laughed. Did we hear the rustle of Emma

Hamilton's muslin skirts as she caught the look in the rogue's eye, or the song of the milk-maid in a chequered dairy—or see Sarah Lethieullier lean over the barley-twist stairs by her dolls' house, the pearls at her throat and ribbons in her dark hair? Ford Lord Grey had bent over Monmouth's hand when he came to a scheming friend for shelter, and whispers of the Rye House Plot were stirring. And Lady Henrietta Berkeley, with her laughing reckless eyes, was moving down the stairs . . . what cared she that Tankerville loved her, or dreamed his passion would lead them both to High Court Trial? Within these new-built walls men heard 'Queen Anne is dead' for the first time. The only sound was the ticking of the clock on the wall, which measured time for many of them.

Then the Admiral's voice was heard, and Anne called me—and we three were come into fairyland.

After that, Jean came, and then Richard and John, and John said: 'Gosh!' at once, as soon as he stood in the hall, which summed up the situation. Dr Johnson might have preferred another word, of course, but I doubt if he could have conveyed the meaning with so much brevity.

The Admiral weighed up responsibilities and liabilities soberly. His appointment to the King's Yacht *Victoria and Albert* gave him grounds to feel he could commission Uppark with care. Being a mere woman I was sure that nothing was impossible, and that feats of restoration must be tackled without too much hesitation. The improbable had happened—we had arrived. The impossible would happen—we could succeed.

'You can't do anything to those curtains! You'll have to throw them away.'

'Those curtains' were not going to be thrown away, though they hung like depressing wreaths of damp distressed pink sea-weed, for I was going to mend them. They were *not* going to be thrown away.

Our friends and relations poured down to see us and Uppark. 'Haven't you thrown those curtains away yet?'

Advice can be a little bleak, but has to be received with smiles.

There was a lot to do, for we were never less than twenty in the house, and we had to achieve balance between school-room and household. There were over thirty curtains, each measuring 16 to 18 feet high and 6 feet wide, which could not be let down:

the sight was too shocking. They were made of Italian brocade of 1740, and I knew of no other house which had them.

Our family was blessed with two maiden aunts, of immortal fame, who fulfilled all the Beatitudes for all the family all their lives, and they brought to Uppark one day a little old lady, who taught me how to make soap from a herb called *Saponaria Officinalis*. She smiled at me kindly after she had taken in the magnitude of the restoration needed.

'You can do it, only it needs work,' she said.

A bundle of herbs was sent for from Norfolk. Pascal, the chef, provided a cauldron for the initiation in the old Still-room kitchen. It was impossible not to think of Macbeth's witches as we watched muslin bags bobbing on the seething spring water in the cauldron, but—as the ritual proceeded—my faith knew no bounds as the air became pervaded with the subtle unforgettable scent that filled my nostrils for the first time, and proved to be my novice introduction to the miracles of nature therapy.

The soap was a brown liquid with a meaningful lather, which covered the surface of the copper like a foaming tankard of beer. The scent that arose to eager nostrils was aromatic and rather exciting.

The Prince Regent's bed and a curtain from the Little Parlour were tackled at once. An alarming process of what was called 'loosening the dirt' took place in a big bath. The water turned inkpot black, and dustbin dirt hid the objects of ablution. If the ragged curtain had entered the bath a sorry mess of powdered rags, it emerged looking more than ever like seaweed which had been dragged from the bed of the ocean!

The little old lady was never daunted and was an inspiring teacher. Would she meet her Waterloo over this Stygian mass of weeds, red and dripping? I was relieved to find she appeared quite unmoved. I was reminded of being told to 'Throw your heart over the fence' when it seemed high to me and my pony out hunting.

By the time our lives were once more disrupted by war we had mended and re-hung twenty-eight brocade curtains, three Queen Anne four-poster beds, and a set of chairs, besides much other restoration.

The work of restoration has gone on for thirty years, and new techniques have been developed over this period in applying the Saponaria to textiles which have been sent to Uppark for repair from Europe and America as well as in Britain.

When war came again, and the family dispersed to fight, I remained as a watch-keeper, and the house of Uppark settled down to its own remote solitude. When daylight died on warm summer evenings, and the noise of the coastal guns had lessened to an occasional muttering, the searchlights would cross each other in the sky between the sentinel Scots firs which framed the dancing fingers of a giant marionette in motion. The men who set the dance in motion were very remote: remote, too, were the villages that lay in the folds of the Downs, out of sight and sound.

It needed a man of action to adjust the manning of Uppark, and the Admiral had his work cut out to make woodsmen, gardeners and farm hands meet all demands. The Uppark Guernsey herd provided the most perfect dairy produce ever known. We lived on fallow venison and game, and the gardens achieved great fame for prize-winning fruit, vegetables, honey and figs. The more exotic grapes and bananas gave place to marketing demands, and *Belladonna Atropa*, grown in the Park and harvested once a year, was a paying crop.

In the sunny weather of the first summer at Uppark (1931) I found the manuscripts. There was a faintly musty earthy smell about the old office in the garden, but I was often drawn to it, to sit at the old office table and absorb the peculiar atmosphere of that room.

Two windows to the east let in the sea-green light of close-grown shrubs beyond the narrow gravel path, and in this light the office papers had a faded damp feel as I drew them from pigeon-holes where they had rested for years. The 'wages sheets' were as long as the hours of work on the estate, and in the garden and the farm. Sixpence once covered the price of a pint of beer, a slice of cheese, a box of matches and a slice of bread. There was free kindling and fuel to be collected as sixteen woodsmen worked in the woods and coppices; there was free beer in the Uppark cellars under the vaulted arches, where the barrels rested on the long wooden shelves, and were filled from the mouth of a pipe that brought the beer from the malt house in the courtyard, where it was made, into the cellar along the whole length of the pipe. There was milk for all on the estate.

Epilogue

A loaf of bread was bought for a couple of pence. Basins of dripping were to be had from the cooks and chef from the spits that were used in the old kitchens to roast deer whole before the blazing fire.

On each of these visits to the old office lurked the possibility of a voyage into the unknown; the strokes of the clock would be the only tie to the world that lay beyond the misty green outside the moulded glass panes, while inside the office there was the curious impression of fleeting figures that belonged to olden times at Uppark.

There were candle-grease spots on the little candle shelves of the office table; there was a clay pipe on a tray with an ivory pen-cutter for the quills; there were seals and sealing-wax. The shrubs tapped against the obscured windowpane, a mouse ran under the hearth of the fireplace; the coiled dophins of the carved chimneypiece (who had heard generations of argument in this room) reminded me of the turns and plunges into icy green waters they seemed still to follow. The sunshine flickering through the green light seemed to give them movement. It was all part of the dateless fairy-tale of Uppark.

I sat down beside the fireplace and let my eyes wander over the miscellany of the room. There were many dusty objects lying around and heaped upon each other. It was like the lumber-room of Prince Prigio. Like him, I began to examine them. Each had its own significance as part of a place that breathed a story of its own. There are houses which have soul and spirit, inclined to joy or sorrow; there are places of dignity and grandeur. There are facades of brick and stone that hold images; there are little silent places where, in half-forgotten whispers in dusty corners, the stories of ages find voice.

A large oaken chest lay under garden chairs—garden chairs that had once sheltered under the rose bushes, whose crimson petals lay in the deep pot-pourri jars of the house. Carmine and vivid rose, the petals still possessed the magic of the day they bloomed, and I had often wondered at their fragrance.

The lid of the chest was heavy. There was a mist before my eyes that came not only from the obscured green light from the windows, but from the sudden knowledge that I was looking at the writings of scribes from the XIVth century, describing the rulings by which all the Ford and Fetherstonhaughs had lived and died, bought and sold, had married and mated, had come to man's estates, fought and fined, had hired and harassed their neighbours, and harnessed their estates.

I could hear hautboy and tabor, tenuous trumpets and the lute-string's music, as my fingers touched the yellow parchments of all sizes . . . some secured with green ties, some with faded ribbon and red tape. The shining wood grain of the old chest was smooth and dark inside, but had not prevented the incursions of rats, mice and maggots; damp exuded from the sheepskin parchments, which were covered with the white and green mould of centuries, but there was a sense of excitement that I shall never forget, for I could see to far horizons from my ivory tower, over lands that were enchanted in magic colour and where, in secret places, I could carry the twisted keys to unlock the stored treasures of Uppark.

The window-panes seemed to reflect a pulsing light as what had been submerged for centuries came to light.

No care was spared: warmth and sunlight did their part and gradually by degrees the story unfolded, the parchments recovered. Over a thousand were sorted and calendared, over a thousand voices came to us from the men of the ink-horns, the lawyers bewigged and hoary, from the men of the villages, the Inns of Holborn, the heiresses of many lands, the owners of property in nigh every county of England, the monks of monasteries and abbeys, the assessors, the conveyancers, the debtors, the little men and women, who left their few possessions to family and church. Few could write their own names, but their voices were heard in these papers, and their mark is there. In the name of the King their deeds were recorded and registered; their wishes for posterity, their hopes for new generations, their sufferings in the wars and the losses they sustained for the political reactions of their day.

For more than thirty years the papers and documents have been studied and cherished as the pearl silver chimes of the old clock bell under the cupola have rung out the hours in summer and in winter too at Uppark. For many of the centuries while the earth has been spinning on its axis, the tenuous threads of the lives that live and breathe in the yellow parchments and quiet pictures were alive at Uppark, so subtly woven into the atmosphere of the place that one can feel instinctively a golden quality that gives a glow to rooms and corridors—the charm of changeless time—from the attics to the cellars, from the spiced smells of store-rooms and the subtle fantasia of the housekeeper's closets. There remain echoes of the age before machines: of flying hooves and champing bits, of chamber music and Sodonini's violin; of post-horn and hunting horns, and the hounds in full cry through the bracken and brakes of the Park. And firelight, when the great logs are lit by dancing flames; when into the silent room at twilight the candles are brought and set at the side of the man who quietly reads in the high-shouldered green leather armchair. There was leisure and pleasure in quietness, there was lasting love, and courage in a man's right arm before police were thought of.

In an old house like Uppark the never-dying waves of sounds of the past haunt the silence and echo in the present. The full range of emotions that were born, endured, enjoyed in secret or in joy, survive and revive as the music of another age.

The MSS were calendared, their essence caught in miniature. A presentation exact and clear set out in detail from the repetitive verbiage of scribes of every age from the fourteenth century. To work with the exactitude set out by Lionel Lindsay's example was like adventuring into the seas of centuries with another world pilot.

Lionel's sensitive face was concentrated on the manuscripts spread before him on the table. The sunshine lit up the gold-and-white walls of the old dining room. His eyes would narrow and his voice break off suddenly as he figured out a new discovery . . . 'Sir Matthew's father, another Matthew, son of Cuthbert and his wife, another Sarah, also another heiress . . . '

Sir Matthew, that man of parts and precision, had sat two hundred years ago where Lionel now sat at the dining room table. When Sir Matthew entered into his possession of Uppark in 1746, he hung the portraits of Cuthbert, and Sarah his wife, by Jansen, between the high windows, where they hang to this day.

Research work on documents, papers and deeds goes on. The selective choice cuts the facets of the diamonds to shine in the story of Uppark, where the scenes of the past could still be enacted today without seeming to be inappropriate to the house.

When the western sun lights up the long Red Drawing Room,

in which the Tankervilles and Fetherstonhaughs played back-gammon with the ivory pieces and shakers, at the gaming-table which is set under the Waterford chandelier, it does not seem so very long ago that they sat there in their powdered wigs and long waistcoats, their brocaded coats and lace ruffles. The smell of their snuff is still very distinct as one plays the large red-and-white ivory pieces.

Such is Uppark. Here one finds something of the quality of T. S. Eliot's:

'Time past, time present, and time future . . . '

Index

Index

Jones, Inigo, 50
Jouard, 64

Keene, Henry, 46
Keppel, Mr, 65
Kew, 64
Kip, Johannes, 25, 26

Lade, Sir John, 55
Lascelles, H., 47
Laver, Ben, 57
Leconfield, Lord and Lady, 104
Lee, Dr Arthur, 41
Legge, gamekeeper, 96
Lethieullier, Benjamin, 29, 46, 47
Lethieullier, Sarah, 29
Lewes, 58
Lindsay, Lionel, 113
Longleat, 77, 85
Longstaffe, 27
Loton, Bucky, 100
Louis XVIII, 93
Lumley, Lord, 22, 23
Lyme Regis, 22
Lyon, Francis, 52

MacLean, Dr, 85
Mansfield Park (quoted), 71
Manton, Joseph, 67
Marie Antoinette, 70
Melton Constable, 26
Merton, 61, 62, 63
Mickleham, 88
Middleton, Lord, 59
Miller, Mr, 31, 33
Mirault, 70
Moget, 56
Monmouth, Duke of, 18, 19, 21, 22, 23, 108
Montagu, Mrs, 57
Moore, Thomas, 47
Morpeth, 38
Morrison, Alfred, 53

Naples, 54, 61, 63
Napoleon I, 64, 65, 78, 81, 91, 97
Nash, John, 72, 73
National Trust, 15
Nelson, Lord, 52, 61, 62, 63
Neston, 52
Newcastle, Duke of, 38, 39

Newcastle on Tyne, 26
Newmarket, 21, 57, 58, 68

Ohio, River, 42
Ord, Robert, 38
Oxford, 38, 48, 50

Page, John, 38
Paget, Sir Arthur, 49, 66, 67, 93, 100
Paget, Berkeley, 66
Paget, Charles, 65, 66
Paget, Henry William, 64
Paine, James, 31
Pall Mall, 24
Paris, 49, 70, 82, 91, 93, 95
Parry, Dr, 85
Pasquier, Du, 64
Peachey, James, 38
Peaston, 57
Pelham, Henry, 38
Pellegrini, 93
Penn, Mr, 43
Pepys, Samuel, 34
Petworth, 31
Philadelphia, 45
Pitt, William, 44, 55, 57
Portsmouth, 39, 64, 73, 106
Pyke, Edward, 47
Pyne, Benjamin, 57

Racing Calendar, The, 55
Rainsbury, 26
Repton, George, 73
Repton, Humphry, 15, 34, 69, 71
    letters quoted, 70-90
Repton, Mrs, 86
Richmond, Duke of, 40
Richmond, Duchess of, 91
Ringwood, 22
Rochford, Lord, 42, 45
Rockingham, Lord, 54
Rome, 49
Romford, 77, 83
Rushworth, Mr, 71
Rye House Plot, 21, 108

Saponaria Officinalis, 109
Savile, Mr, 59
Scottish Office, 31
Sedgmoor, Battle of, 22
Sefton, Lady, 67

117